HARCOURT

Math

Challenge
Workbook

TEACHER EDITION
Grade 6

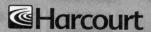

Harcourt

Orlando   Austin   Chicago   New York   Toronto   London   San Diego

Visit *The Learning Site!*
www.harcourtschool.com

REPRODUCING COPIES FOR STUDENTS

This Teacher's Edition contains full-size student pages
with answers printed in non-reproducible blue ink.

It may be necessary to adjust the exposure control on
your photocopy machine to a lighter setting to ensure
that blue answers do not reproduce.

Printed in the United States of America

ISBN 0-15-336521-8

2 3 4 5 6 7 8 9 10 054 10 09 08 07 06 05 04

CONTENTS

Gazillions of Numbers

The chart below lists the names of some very large numbers. Use the chart to answer the questions that follow.

million	1,000,000	undecillion	1 followed by 36 zeros
billion	1,000,000,000	duodecillion	1 followed by 39 zeros
trillion	1,000,000,000,000	tredecillion	1 followed by 42 zeros
quadrillion	1,000,000,000,000,000	quattuordecillion	1 followed by 45 zeros
quintillion	1,000,000,000,000,000,000	quindecillion	1 followed by 48 zeros
sextillion	1 followed by 21 zeros	sexdecillion	1 followed by 51 zeros
septillion	1 followed by 24 zeros	septendecillion	1 followed by 54 zeros
octillion	1 followed by 27 zeros	octodecillion	1 followed by 57 zeros
nonillion	1 followed by 30 zeros	novemdecillion	1 followed by 60 zeros
decillion	1 followed by 33 zeros	vigintillion	1 followed by 63 zeros

1. How many zeros are added to create each new number in the chart?

   3 zeros

2. What is the name of the number equal to 1,000 trillion?

   1 quadrillion

3. What is the name of the number equal to 1,000 octodecillion?

   1 novemdecillion

4. How many zeros would there be in 100 septendecillion?

   56 zeros

5. In one year, light travels about 6 trillion miles. Write this number in standard form.

   6,000,000,000,000

6. There are more than two hundred quintillion stars in the universe. How would you write this number in standard form?

   200 followed by 18 zeros

7. A galaxy called the Large Magellanic Cloud is 950,000,000,000,000,000 miles from Earth. Write the word form of this number.

   nine hundred fifty quadrillion

8. A googol is a 1 followed by 100 zeros. How many zeros are there in 10 googol?

   101 zeros

Name _____

Estimating Populations

POPULATION OF THE MIDDLE COLONIES: 1670 – 1750					
Colony	1670	1690	1710	1730	1750
Delaware	700	1,482	3,645	9,170	28,704
New Jersey	1,000	8,000	19,872	35,510	71,393
New York	5,754	13,909	21,625	48,594	76,696
Pennsylvania	—	11,450	24,450	51,707	119,666

The table shows how the population of the middle colonies changed from 1670 to 1750. Use the table to answer the questions. Estimate to the nearest thousand.

1. About how many people lived in Delaware and New York, in total, in 1690?

   about 15,000 people

2. About how many people lived in Pennsylvania and New Jersey, in total, in 1730?

   about 88,000 people

3. About how many more people lived in New York than in Delaware in 1710?

   about 18,000 more people

4. About how many more people lived in Pennsylvania in 1750 than in 1690?

   about 109,000 more people

5. About how many people lived in the middle colonies in 1670?

   about 8,000 people

6. About how many people lived in the middle colonies in 1750?

   about 297,000 people

7. About how many more people lived in the middle colonies in 1750 than in 1670?

   about 289,000 more people

At the Airport

The table shows the number of passengers at five airports in 2000 and the approximate area of each airport.

Airport	Number of Passengers	Area (in acres)
Phoenix International	35,890,000	3,000
Orlando International	30,823,000	15,000
Denver International	38,749,000	34,000
Baltimore/Washington International	19,700,000	3,600
Atlanta International	80,171,000	3,750

1. Estimate the total number of passengers who used the Atlanta and Denver airports during 2000.

    _____ Possible answer: about 119,000,000 passengers

2. Which airport had the fewest passengers?

    _____ Baltimore/Washington

3. What was the total number of passengers who used these five airports during 2000?

    _____ 205,333,000 passengers

4. How many more passengers used the Denver airport than used the Phoenix airport?

    _____ 2,859,000 more passengers

5. Which airport had more than forty million passengers in 2000?

    _____ Atlanta

6. Orlando International had more passengers than Baltimore/ Washington International. How do their areas compare?

    _____ Orlando International is 11,400 acres larger.

7. Find the difference in area between the largest airport and the smallest airport.

    _____ 31,000 acres

8. What is the total area of these five airports?

    _____ 59,350 acres

Number Crossword

Solve each problem. Use the answers to complete the puzzle.

Across

1. $1,685 \times 124 =$ _____208,940_____

2. $65 \times 104 =$ _____6,760_____

3. $2,549 \times 317 =$ _____808,033_____

4. $596 \times 240 =$ _____143,040_____

5. $99 \times 5 =$ _____495_____

6. $6,058 \times 847 =$ _____5,131,126_____

7. $351 \times 208 =$ _____73,008_____

8. $872 \times 234 =$ _____204,048_____

Down

1. $6,150 \div 3 =$ _____2,050_____

4. $3,454 \div 22 =$ _____157_____

5. $855 \div 19 =$ _____45_____

9. $25,344 \div 36 =$ _____704_____

10. $16,740 \div 54 =$ _____310_____

11. $7,968 \div 16 =$ _____498_____

12. $46,295 \div 47 =$ _____985_____

13. $17,568 \div 36 =$ _____488_____

14. $14,761 \div 29 =$ _____509_____

15. $32,625 \div 87 =$ _____375_____

16. $9,672 \div 93 =$ _____104_____

17. $7,896 \div 12 =$ _____658_____

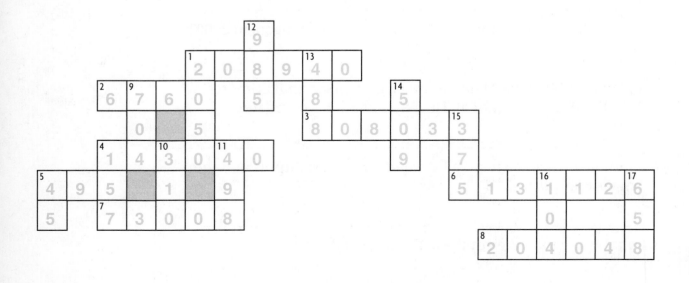

Patterns, Patterns

Draw the next three possible figures of the pattern. Then describe the rule used to form the pattern. Possible answers are given.

1. ◣ ☐ ◣ ◣ ☐ ☐ ◣ ◣ ◣   ☐ ☐ ☐

Rule: _____ Triangle, square, then repeat adding one _____

_____ triangle and one square, repeating _____

2. ○ ☐ ◇ ◇ ☐ ○ ○ ☐ ◇   ◇ ☐ ○

Rule: _____ Circle, square, diamond, then reverse _____

_____

3. ○ ◇ ○ ☐ ◇ ☐ ○ ◇ ○   ☐ ◇ ☐

Rule: _____ Circle, diamond, circle, then replace circles with _____

_____ squares, then back to circle, diamond, circle, repeating _____

4. ◰ ◧ ■ ■ ◨ ◳ ◲ ◨ ■   ■ ◧ ◰

Rule: _____ Square 1/4 shaded, square 1/2 shaded, square _____

_____ entirely shaded, then reverse _____

Give the next three numbers in the pattern. Then describe the rule.

5. 1, 2, 4, 8, 16, 32, _64_, _128_, _256_, . . .

Rule: _____ Multiply by 2. _____

6. 3, 2, 4, 3, 5, 4, _6_, _5_, _7_, . . .

Rule: _____ Subtract 1, add 2. _____

7. 3, 6, 9, 15, 24, 39, _63_, _102_, _165_, . . .

Rule: _____ Add the two previous terms. _____

Name _____

Expression Match

Write an algebraic expression for "a number, *n*, less than seven, all divided by 2."

$(7 - n) \div 2$

- The 7 must come first, because *n* is less than 7.
- To show "all divided by 2," use parentheses.

Draw a line connecting the word expression in Column 1 to the correct algebraic expression in Column 2.

Column 1	Column 2
1. twenty-two less than a number, *a*, all times three	A. $a \div 3 + 22$
2. twenty-two times a number, *a*, plus three	B. $a - 3 + 22$
3. a number, *a*, increased by three, all times twenty-two	C. $22 \times a + 3$
4. a number, *a*, decreased by twenty-two, all divided by three	D. $(a - 22) \times 3$
5. twenty-two times a number, *a*, decreased by three	E. $(22 - a) \times 3$
6. a number, *a*, divided by three, increased by twenty-two	F. $(a - 22) \div 3$
7. the sum of three and twenty-two, all divided by a number, *a*	G. $(a + 3) \div 22$
8. a number, *a*, less than twenty-two, all times three	H. $(a + 3) \times 22$
9. the sum of a number, *a*, and three, all divided by twenty-two.	I. $22 \times a - 3$
10. a number, *a*, decreased by three and then increased by twenty-two	J. $(3 + 22) \div a$

Solve the Clues!

Use mental math to solve each equation clue. Find the answer in the Tip Box below. Write the letter of that equation above it. When you have solved all the equations, you will have discovered a math tip that is especially important when solving equations.

Clues

A	$12a = 96$	_8_	**N**	$n \div 4 = 100$	_400_
B	$b - 10 = 1$	_11_	**O**	$o - 8 = 16 + 12$	_36_
C	$c \div 3 = 5$	_15_	**P**	$p \times 2 = 700$	_350_
D	$12 + d = 12$	_0_	**R**	$7 \times 36 = r \times 14$	_18_
E	$4e = 20$	_5_	**S**	$s \div 10 = 41$	_410_
G	$8g = 320$	_40_	**T**	$t + 83 = 289$	_206_
H	$7 + 9 + h = 80$	_64_	**U**	$u \times 184 = 184$	_1_
I	$28 + i = 47$	_19_	**W**	$9 \times 16 = w \times 12$	_12_
K	$2k = 100$	_50_	**X**	$x - 17 = 29$	_46_
L	$300 = l - 75$	_375_	**Y**	$5y = 1,000$	_200_

Tip Box

A	L	W	A	Y	S		C	H	E	C	K		Y	O	U	R
8	375	12	8	200	410		15	64	5	15	50		200	36	1	18

A	N	S	W	E	R		T	O		B	E		S	U	R	E
8	400	410	12	5	18		206	36		11	5		410	1	18	5

I	T		I	S		C	O	R	R	E	C	T	.
19	206		19	410		15	36	18	18	5	15	206	

Use your answers to solve the riddle.

Riddle: Which football bowl game do flies like best?

T	H	E		S	U	G	A	R		B	O	W	L
206	64	5		410	1	40	8	18		11	36	12	375

Name _____

The Missing Equation

Write an equation to illustrate each property in the chart. Both sides
of the equation must be equal to the number given in the value column.
The first one is done for you. Possible answers are given.

EQUATION	PROPERTY	VALUE
$7 \times 6 = 6 \times 7$	Commutative Property of Multiplication	42
$16 + 25 = 25 + 16$	Commutative Property of Addition	41
$2 \times (10 + 9) = (2 \times 10) + (2 \times 9)$	Distributive Property	38
$1{,}458 \times 1 = 1 \times 1{,}458$	Identity Property of Multiplication	1,458
$12 + 0 = 0 + 12$	Identity Property of Addition	12
$4 \times (13 + 8) = (4 \times 13) + (4 \times 8)$	Distributive Property	84
$377 + 472 = 472 + 377$	Commutative Property of Addition	849
$8 \times (15 + 15) = (8 \times 15) + (8 \times 15)$	Distributive Property	240
$(13 + 17) + 35 = 13 + (17 + 35)$	Associative Property of Addition	65
$27 \times 4 = 4 \times 27$	Commutative Property of Multiplication	108
$(2 \times 3) \times 9 = 2 \times (3 \times 9)$	Associative Property of Multiplication	54
$64{,}141 + 0 = 0 + 64{,}141$	Identity Property of Addition	64,141
$2.79 \times 1 = 1 \times 2.79$	Identity Property of Multiplication	2.79
$(9 \times 3) \times 19 = 9 \times (3 \times 19)$	Associative Property of Multiplication	513

© Harcourt

CW8   Challenge

Solve It

Use mental math to solve each problem in the Decoder Box. Find the value in the Tip Box. Each time the value appears, write the letter of that problem above it. When you have solved all the problems, you will have discovered the math tip.

Decoder Box

A	$63 + 27 =$	90	**N**	$13 \times 6 =$	78
B	$112 - 14 =$	98	**O**	$4 \times 11 \times 3 =$	132
C	$480 \div 8 =$	60	**P**	$198 \div 9 =$	22
D	$6 \times 7 \times 10 =$	420	**Q**	$5 + 34 + 4 =$	43
E	$55 \times 3 =$	165	**R**	$15 \times 4 \times 2 =$	120
F	$397 - 158 =$	239	**S**	$16 \times 7 =$	112
H	$2 \times 13 \times 5 =$	130	**T**	$25 \times 6 =$	150
I	$7 \times 21 =$	147	**U**	$440 \div 5 =$	88
K	$803 - 571 =$	232	**V**	$25 + 19 + 4 =$	48
L	$9 \times 2 \times 6 =$	108	**Y**	$197 + 326 =$	523
M	$8 \times 5 \times 4 =$	160	**Z**	$1,135 - 797 =$	338

Tip Box

F	A	C	T	O	R	S		C	A	N		B	E
239	90	60	150	132	120	112		60	90	78		98	165

M	U	L	T	I	P	L	I	E	D		I	N
160	88	108	150	147	22	108	147	165	420		147	78

A	N	Y		O	R	D	E	R
90	78	523		132	120	420	165	120

Now use the Decoder Box to help you find the answer to a riddle.

What is useful only when it's used up?

A	N		U	M	B	R	E	L	L	A
90	78		88	160	98	120	165	108	108	90

Puzzling Exponents

Complete the puzzle with the values.

		¹1	3	3	²1			⁴2	8	9						
³1	2	5			0											
⁵3		6		⁶2	4	0	1				⁷1					
4		⁸2	7	⁹4	4		¹⁰6	5	6	¹¹1	2					
¹²3	1	¹³2	5		0		¹⁴9			7	9					
	1		¹⁵1	0	0	0	0		¹⁶2	5	6					
	8				0			¹⁷1	2	8						
¹⁸3	3	7	¹⁹5													
			7													
			6													

Across

1. 11^3
3. 5^3
4. 17^2
6. 7^4
8. 14^3
10. 9^4
12. 5^5
15. 10^4
16. 16^2
17. 2^7
18. 15^3

Down

1. 25^3
2. 2^{10}
4. 6^3
5. 7^3
7. 6^4
9. 20^2
11. 12^3
13. 3^7
14. 30^2
19. 24^2

Order Counts!

Parentheses can change the value of an expression, as can the order of operations within the expression.

$$6 + 6 \times 6 - 6 = 36 \qquad \text{but} \qquad 6 + 6 \times (6 - 6) = 6$$

1. Simplify $(3 + 3) \times 3 + 3 \div 3$. _____19_____

2. Use five 3s to write an expression whose value is 5.

   Possible answer: $3 \div 3 + 3 \div 3 + 3$

3. Use five 3s to write an expression whose value is 3.

   Possible answer: $3 \times 3 \div 3 + 3 - 3$

Use parentheses and exponents.

4. Use five 3s to write an expression whose value is 27.

   Possible answer: $(3 + 3) \times 3 + 3 \times 3$

5. Use five 3s to write an expression whose value is 29.

   Possible answer: $(3 + 3) \div 3 + 3^3$

6. Use five 3s to write an expression whose value is 0 or 1.

   Possible answers: $3 \times 3 - (3 + 3 + 3); (3 - 3)^3 + 3 \div 3$

Place one or more sets of parentheses in the expression on the left side of each equation so that the resulting equation is true.

7. $5 - 2 \times 4 + 3 = 15$

   $(5 - 2) \times 4 + 3 = 15$

8. $6 + 1^2 - 20 = 29$

   $(6 + 1)^2 - 20 = 29$

9. $3 + 2 \times 7 - 5 = 10$

   $(3 + 2) \times (7 - 5) = 10$

10. $4 + 1 \times 6 - 2 = 20$

    $(4 + 1) \times (6 - 2) = 20$

11. $11 + 6 - 3^2 = 20$

    $11 + (6 - 3)^2 = 20$

12. $64 \div 4 \times 4 - 1 + 1 = 2$

    $64 \div (4 \times 4) - (1 + 1) = 2$

Use each of the numbers 4, 6, 8, and 10 once to make a true expression.

13. $(\underline{8} \times \underline{4}) + (\underline{6} \times \underline{10}) = 92$

14. $\underline{10} \div (\underline{8} - \underline{6}) + \underline{4} = 9$

15. $(\underline{10} + \underline{4}) - (\underline{6} + \underline{8}) = 0$

16. $(\underline{10} + \underline{8}) - (\underline{6} + \underline{4}) = 8$

Multistep Riddles

Solve these riddles. Each one will take several steps.

1. I am a five-digit number.
   My ones digit is the sum of my tens and ten-thousands digits.
   My tens digit is the sum of my hundreds and ten-thousands digits.
   My hundreds digit is the sum of my thousands digit and my ten-thousands digit.
   My thousands digit is 1 more than my ten-thousands digit.
   My ten-thousands digit is 1.

   What number am I? _____ 12,345 _____

   How did you solve the riddle? _____ Possible answer: Work backward _____
   _____ from the last clue. _____

2. The makers of Crinkle Crackers had a special offer:
   "Collect 8 labels and get 1 bag free." Jim asked his
   friends for their labels. He collected 85 labels in all.

   How many free bags of Crinkle Crackers did he get? _____ 12 _____

   How did you solve the riddle? Possible answer: Jim got 10 free bags with
   the 85 labels and had 5 labels left over. Each of the 10 free bags had a
   label, so he used 8 of those to get another free bag. With that bag's label
   and the 7 labels he had left over, Jim got his twelfth bag.

3. Margarite has 21 bottles. Seven bottles are full of juice. Seven
   bottles contain no juice at all. Three of the bottles are half-full,
   and four of them are half-empty.

   Margarite wants to divide the juice among herself, her sister, and
   her brother. Each person will receive the same number of bottles
   and an equal amount of juice.

   No juice will be poured from one bottle to another. No one will
   have more than 3 bottles of the same kind—full, empty, half-full,
   or half-empty. Complete the table to show how Margarite divides
   her bottles of juice. Possible answer is given.

	Full	Empty	Half-full	Half-empty
Margarite	3	3	1	0
Sister	2	2	2	1
Brother	2	2	0	3

   How did you solve the riddle? _____ Possible answer: There are _____
   _____ $(7 + 0 + 1.5 + 2) \div 3 = 3.5$ bottles of juice per person. _____

Comparing Scoring Leaders

SCORING LEADERS	
Player	Average
Elgin Baylor	27.4
Wilt Chamberlain	30.1
George Gervin	26.2
Bob Pettit	26.4
Oscar Robertson	25.7
Jerry West	27.0
Dominique Wilkins	24.8

The table above shows the scoring averages of some retired NBA scoring leaders. Use the table for 1—8.

1. Which of the players listed in the table has the greatest average?

   Wilt Chamberlain

2. Which of the players listed in the table has the least average?

   Dominique Wilkins

3. Use the symbol > to list the averages of Oscar Robertson, George Gervin, and Bob Pettit from greatest to least.

   26.4 > 26.2 > 25.7

4. Use the symbol < to list all of the averages shown in the table from least to greatest.

   24.8 < 25.7 < 26.2 < 26.4 < 27.0 < 27.4 < 30.1

5. Michael Jordan's scoring average was 31.5. Where would he be placed in the list you made for Exercise 4?

   after Wilt Chamberlain (30.1)

6. Through the 1998-1999 season, Karl Malone's scoring average was 26.1. Where would he be placed in the list you made for Exercise 4?

   after Oscar Robertson (25.7) but before George Gervin (26.2)

7. Which player in the table had an average greater than 25.5 but less than 26.0?

   Oscar Robertson

8. Which players in the table had an average greater than 26.0 but less than 28.0?

   Elgin Baylor, George Gervin, Bob Pettit, Jerry West

© Harcourt

Name _____

Come Fly with Me!

In 1995, about 47,000,000 visitors arrived in the United States by airplane. This was about 4,000,000 more than the number of Americans who traveled by airplane from the United States to other countries. Some of the countries from which the greatest number of visitors came were Canada (7,262,000), France (2,045,000), Germany (3,125,000), Japan (5,676,000), Mexico (4,884,000), and the United Kingdom (6,648,000).

Complete the table below, ordering the countries from the greatest number of visitors to the United States to the least number. Then solve Problems 1–6.

Airline Passenger Arrivals in the United States	
Country	Number of Visitors
Canada	7,262,000
United Kingdom	6,648,000
Japan	5,676,000
Mexico	4,884,000
Germany	3,125,000
France	2,045,000

1. Approximately how many Americans left the United States by

   airplane to visit other countries in 1995? ___about 43,000,000 Americans___

2. From which two countries did the greatest number of visitors come?

   _____Canada and the United Kingdom_____

3. About how many total visitors were there from these two countries?

   _____about 14,000,000 visitors_____

4. About how many visitors flew to the United States from countries other than those included in the table?

   _____Possible answer: about 17,000,000 visitors_____

5. In 1995, about 1,580,000 people flew to the United States from the Netherlands. About how many fewer people came from the Netherlands than from the last country listed in the table?

   _____Possible answer: about 500,000 visitors_____

6. About three times as many visitors flew to the United States from France in 1995 as flew here in 1990. Approximately how many visitors flew to the United States from France in 1990?

   _____Possible answer: about 700,000 visitors_____

Estimate with Decimals

Play the following game with a friend.

For each problem, both players record an estimate for the value that should be placed in the blank in the given mathematical sentence. The winner of each round is the player whose estimate is closer to the actual value.

For example, in the problem $48.23 +$ _____ $= 198.2$, each player chooses a number he or she believes can be added to 48.23 to give a sum close to 198.2. After each player has recorded a number, both solve the problem to find that the actual value is 149.97. The player whose estimate is closer to the value wins the round.

For Exercises 1–8, students' responses will vary.

1. $6.3 \times$ _____ $= 53.9$

   Player 1's estimate _____ Player 2's estimate _____ Winner _____

2. $9.1 + 3.2 + 5.6 +$ _____ $= 22.8$

   Player 1's estimate _____ Player 2's estimate _____ Winner _____

3. $76.2 \div$ _____ $= 10.1$

   Player 1's estimate _____ Player 2's estimate _____ Winner _____

4. $155.2 -$ _____ $= 54.9$

   Player 1's estimate _____ Player 2's estimate _____ Winner _____

5. $220.5 + 186.3 + 94.1 +$ _____ $= 800.8$

   Player 1's estimate _____ Player 2's estimate _____ Winner _____

6. $17.5 \times$ _____ $= 240$

   Player 1's estimate _____ Player 2's estimate _____ Winner _____

7. $462.8 \div$ _____ $= 89.2$

   Player 1's estimate _____ Player 2's estimate _____ Winner _____

8. _____ $- 64.78 = 97.63$

   Player 1's estimate _____ Player 2's estimate _____ Winner _____

Name _____

Decimals and Percents

Shady Dealings

Shade each grid according to the given rule. Then answer the questions. For Exercises 1–4 and 6, sample shadings are given.

1. Shade the grid so there are 10 more shaded squares than unshaded squares.

   What percent of the grid is shaded and what percent of the grid is unshaded?

   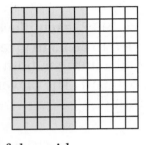

   _____ 55%; 45% _____

2. Shade the grid so there are 30 more unshaded squares than shaded squares.

   What percent of the grid is shaded and what percent of the grid is unshaded?

   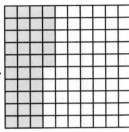

   _____ 35%; 65% _____

3. Shade the grid so that the unshaded part is one-fourth the size of the shaded part. What percent of the grid is shaded and what percent of the grid is unshaded?

   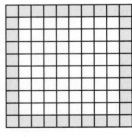

   _____ 80%; 20% _____

4. Shade the grid so that the unshaded part is three times the size of the shaded part. What decimal names the part of the grid that is shaded? Unshaded?

   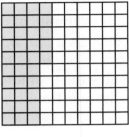

   _____ 0.25; 0.75 _____

5. Shade every square that touches the outside of the grid. What decimal names the part of the grid that is shaded?

   _____ 0.36 _____

   What percent of the grid is unshaded?

   _____ 64% _____

6. Shade the grid so that if one more square is shaded, then the number of shaded squares would be 20 greater than the number of unshaded squares. What percent of the grid is shaded and what percent of the grid is unshaded?

   _____ 59%; 41% _____

© Harcourt

CW16 Challenge

Name _____

LESSON 4.1

Pattern Practice

Identify the addition or subtraction rule that was used to create each pattern. Then name the next three decimals.

1. 94.8, 94.3, 92.8, 90.3, _86.8_, _82.3_, _76.8_ . . .

   Rule: _Subtract 0.5, then 1.5, then 2.5, and so on._

2. 54.95, 56.06, 58.28, 61.61, _66.05_, _71.6_, _78.26_ . . .

   Rule: _Add 1.11, then 2.22, then 3.33, and so on._

3. 52.3, 50.2, 48, 45.7, _43.3_, _40.8_, _38.2_ . . .

   Rule: _Subtract 2.1, then 2.2, then 2.3, then 2.4, and so on._

4. 27.5, 26, 23.5, 22, _19.5_, _18_, _15.5_ . . .

   Rule: _Subtract 1.5, then 2.5, then 1.5, and so on._

5. 64.23, 69.93, 74.73, 80.43, _85.23_, _90.93_, _95.73_ . . .

   Rule: _Add 5.7, then 4.8, then 5.7, and so on._

6. 12.72, 22.71, 31.59, 39.36, _46.02_, _51.57_, _56.01_ . . .

   Rule: _Add 9.99, then 8.88, then 7.77, and so on._

7. 815.634, 803.289, 748.968, 736.623, _682.302_, _669.957_, _615.636_ . . .

   Rule: _Subtract 12.345, then 54.321, then 12.345, and so on._

8. 28.003, 34.249, 42.448, 48.694, _56.893_, _63.139_, _71.338_ . . .

   Rule: _Add 6.246, then 8.199, then 6.246, and so on._

9. 38.15, 35.25, 40.65, 37.75, _43.15_, _40.25_, _45.65_ . . .

   Rule: _Subtract 2.9, then add 5.4, then subtract 2.9, and so on._

10. Make up two pattern problems of your own. Exchange papers with a classmate and solve. Check students' work.

   _____

   _____

© Harcourt

Challenge CW17

Puzzling Problems

Find each product. Locate the product in the Tip Box. (Hint: Not all products are in the Tip Box.) Each place where the product appears, write the letter of the exercise above it. When you have solved all the problems, you will discover a math tip for multiplying decimals.

A	5.26 × 7.5 = _39.45_	**N**	2.008 × 1.2 = _2.4096_
B	0.12 × 1.2 = _0.144_	**O**	6.1 × 0.42 = _2.562_
C	3 × 0.009 = _0.027_	**P**	0.54 × 2.9 = _1.566_
D	2.9 × 2.03 = _5.887_	**R**	0.3 × 30 = _9_
E	8 × 2.5 = _20_	**S**	1.8 × 2.3 = _4.14_
G	0.15 × 0.07 = _0.0105_	**T**	6 × 1.7 = _10.2_
H	7.4 × 6.8 = _50.32_	**U**	5.9 × 0.04 = _0.236_
I	0.04 × 40.5 = _1.62_	**V**	8.5 × 6.3 = _53.55_
J	0.25 × 3.8 = _0.95_	**W**	46.7 × 2.3 = _107.41_
M	190 × 0.03 = _5.7_		

Tip Box

R	E	M	E	M	B	E	R
9	20	5.7	20	5.7	0.144	20	9

T	O		E	S	T	I	M	A	T	E
10.2	2.562		20	4.14	10.2	1.62	5.7	39.45	10.2	20

T	H	E		P	R	O	D	U	C	T.
10.2	50.32	20		1.566	9	2.562	5.887	0.236	0.027	10.2

Name _____

Missing Digits

Complete each division problem by writing the missing digits in the boxes.

1.

```
            3 . 8 7
      ┌──────────────
    5 │ 1   9 . 3   5
      - 1   5
        ───
          4   3
        - 4   0
          ───
              3   5
            - 3   5
              ───
                  0
```

2.

```
             0 . 6   5
       ┌────────────────
    21 │ 1  3 . 6   5
                0
            ─────
          1   3   6
        - 1   2   6
          ─────────
              1   0   5
            - 1   0   5
              ─────────
                      0
```

3.

```
            3 . 2   8
       ┌──────────────
    26 │ 8  5 . 2   8
        7   8
        ─────
          7   2
        - 5   2
          ─────
            2   0   8
          - 2   0   8
            ─────────
                    0
```

4.

```
           2   7 . 4
      ┌────────────────
    8 │ 2  1   9 . 2
        1   6
        ─────
          5   9
        - 5   6
          ─────
              3   2
            - 3   2
              ─────
                  0
```

Name _____

Decimal Solutions

Find each quotient. Locate the quotient in the Tip Box. (Hint: Not all quotients are in the Tip Box.) Each place where the quotient appears, write the letter of the exercise above it. When you have solved all the problems, you will discover a math tip for dividing decimals.

A	$6.3 \div 0.05 =$	126	**N** $9.3 \div 0.6 =$	15.5
B	$50.2 \div 0.01 =$	5,020	**O** $0.0024 \div 0.3 =$	0.008
C	$33.6 \div 8 =$	4.2	**P** $8.7 \div 17.4 =$	0.5
E	$5.4 \div 0.02 =$	270	**Q** $28.7 \div 8.2 =$	3.5
F	$107.91 \div 5.5 =$	19.62	**R** $400.98 \div 24.6 =$	16.3
G	$4.077 \div 0.18 =$	22.65	**S** $21.54 \div 0.6 =$	35.9
H	$9 \div 0.3 =$	30	**T** $0.4168 \div 8 =$	0.0521
I	$1.6 \div 0.4 =$	4	**U** $25 \div 0.005 =$	5,000
K	$5.44 \div 1.7 =$	3.2	**W** $0.568 \div 0.4 =$	1.42
L	$0.192 \div 0.3 =$	0.64	**Y** $4.48 \div 0.08 =$	56
M	$8.05 \div 0.7 =$	11.5	**Z** $6.3 \div 0.18 =$	35

Tip Box

M	U	L	T	I	P	L	Y		T	O
11.5	5,000	0.64	0.0521	4	0.5	0.64	56		0.0521	0.008

C	H	E	C	K		T	H	E
4.2	30	270	4.2	3.2		0.0521	30	270

A	N	S	W	E	R
126	15.5	35.9	1.42	270	16.3 .

© Harcourt

Interpret the Remainder

In each problem, explain the mistake in reasoning that was made.
Describe how the mistake might have been avoided. Possible answers given.

1. All 159 sixth grade students at McKinley Middle School and their
   7 teachers are going on a trip. The principal ordered 5 buses that
   could each carry 31 passengers. He planned to use a school van
   that could carry 8 passengers as transportation for those people
   who would not have seats on the buses.

   The 5 buses could carry 155 of the 166 people, leaving 11 people, not 8.

   The principal could have planned for 6 buses instead.

2. A farmer is putting up a new fence that will measure 64 feet long.
   He wants to place fence posts 8 feet apart, beginning at one end,
   to support the fencing. He orders 8 fence posts.

   The farmer needs 9, not 8, posts. Instead of dividing 64 by 8, he could

   have drawn a diagram to find the number of posts needed.

3. Margo and her sister have $10.00 to spend on cards. The cards
   Margo has chosen cost $0.95 each. She tells her sister they can
   buy 11 cards with the money they have. They stand in line to pay
   for the 11 cards.

   Margo and her sister do not have enough money. $10.00 divided by

   $0.95 is 10 r50. The remainder means they only have $0.50 left. This

   is not enough to buy another card.

4. Eighty-five teenagers have come to register for a new baseball
   league. Each team will have 9 members. The organizers of the
   league tell the teens that as soon as 4 more people arrive, they will
   have exactly enough players for everyone to be assigned to a team.

   85 ÷ 9 = 9 r4; The organizers thought the remainder meant 4 more

   players were needed, but the remainder meant those not on a team.

   So, 5 more players are needed.

Match Up

Match each description with its expression.

1. The cost of 3 shirts and 2 sweaters if each shirt costs s dollars and each sweater costs w dollars

   f _____

2. The difference between the distances traveled on 3 days of driving and 2 days of walking if the distance driven each day is s miles, the distance walked each day is w miles, and s is greater than w

   d _____

3. The total number of hours studied if you study s hours for 2 weeks and w hours for 3 weeks

   e _____

4. The total distance run in training for a race if you run w miles per week for 3 weeks

   c _____

5. The price paid for one apple if you pay w dollars for 3 apples

   a _____

6. The difference between the greater amount you will earn in May if you work 3 weeks earning w dollars per week and the amount you will earn in June if you work 2 weeks earning s dollars per week

   j _____

7. The total number of pages you study if you study 3 pages per hour for w hours and one page per hour for s hours

   h _____

8. The price you pay for one container of juice and one container of milk if juice costs w dollars for 3 containers and milk costs s dollars per container

   b _____

9. The number of miles you can drive on 3 tanks of gas if your car averages s miles per tankful

   g _____

10. The cost of 2 entrees and 1 salad at a restaurant if each entree costs w dollars and salads cost s dollars for 3 salads

    k _____

a. $\dfrac{w}{3}$

b. $\dfrac{w}{3} + s$

c. $3w$

d. $3s - 2w$

e. $2s + 3w$

f. $3s + 2w$

g. $3s$

h. $3w + s$

j. $3w - 2s$

k. $2w + \dfrac{s}{3}$

More Samples

In a **random sample**, each member of the population has an equal chance of being selected.

In a **stratified sample**, the population is classified into at least two different classes, or strata, with the same characteristics, such as male and female. Then another method, such as random sampling, is used to select members of each class.

In a **systematic sample**, every *n*th member from a list is selected. Selecting every fiftieth name from a telephone book is an example of systematic sampling.

In a **cluster sample**, the population is divided into sections, and several sections are randomly selected. Then all the members from the chosen sections are selected.

Identify the type of sampling used as a *random sample*, a *stratified sample*, a *systematic sample*, or a *cluster sample*.

1. A coach selects every fourth student in a class to run a mile.

   _____ systematic sample

2. A principal selects 25 boys and 25 girls from the sixth grade.

   _____ stratified sample

3. A teacher selects all the students in 5 randomly selected classes.

   _____ cluster sample

4. A student writes the names of all her classmates on cards, mixes the cards, and then draws 4 of the cards.

   _____ random sample

5. A teacher selects children under the age of 10 and over the age of 10 from an elementary school

   _____ stratified sample

6. A parent selects every tenth family member from a list of students' family members.

   _____ systematic sample

7. A teacher selects every student in the cafeteria during randomly selected lunch times.

   _____ cluster sample

8. A reporter interviews 10 children from each of the grades in an elementary school.

   _____ stratified sample

Name _____

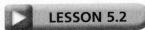

Bias in Advertising

Most advertisements try to persuade consumers to buy certain products. Some advertisements use biased surveys to make their products seem better than any others. Look carefully at advertisements shown in magazines and newspapers. Find an ad that includes either a biased question or a biased survey to promote a product. Answer these questions about the ad. Answers will vary.

1. What product does the advertisement feature? _____

_____

2. How is the question or survey biased? _____

_____

_____

_____

3. How does the bias make the product seem appealing? _____

_____

_____

_____

4. Describe two ways that the question or survey could be changed

   to eliminate the bias. _____

_____

_____

_____

5. Explain why recognizing bias in advertisements will help you

   become a smart shopper. _____

_____

_____

© Harcourt

CW24   **Challenge**

Video Game Survey

Marla surveyed sixth-grade students about the number of hours per week they spend playing video games. She organized her data in the cumulative frequency table and line plot below. Use the table and line plot to answer the questions.

Hours Sixth Graders Spent Playing Video Games Each Week		
Number of Hours	Frequency	Cumulative Frequency
0	14	14
1	6	20
2	9	29
3	7	36
4	5	41
5	6	47
6	3	50

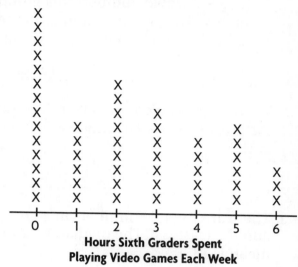

Hours Sixth Graders Spent
Playing Video Games Each Week

1. How many students did Marla survey?

   50 students

2. What is the range of her data?

   6

3. What fraction of the students surveyed spend 4 hours a week playing video games?

   $\frac{1}{10}$ of the students

4. What fraction of the students surveyed spend less than 2 hours a week playing video games?

   $\frac{2}{5}$ of the students

5. What fraction of the students surveyed spend more than 3 hours a week playing video games?

   $\frac{7}{25}$ of the students

6. For every 1 student who responded "6 hours," there were 2 students who responded "5 hours." What other pair of responses has a similar relationship?

   (1:2 ratio) 3 hr:0 hr; 6 hr:1 hr

7. Suppose Marla continued the survey and polled 100 additional classmates. Based on her first survey, how many students would likely respond "0 hours"?

   42 students

8. Suppose Marla wanted to expand her survey and ask another question about video game play. What are two possible questions she might ask?

   Possible answers: What is your favorite game? What type of system do you have?

Number Puzzles

Use the information to find the numbers in the group. The first one is done for you. Possible answers are given.

1. There are 7 whole numbers in a group. The least number in the group is 6. The greatest number in the group is 16. The mode of the group is 15. The median is 10 and the mean is 11.

   _____ 6, 7, 8, 10, 15, 15, 16 _____

2. There are 5 whole numbers in a group. The least number is 7 and the greatest is 14. The mode is 9 and the median is 9. The mean is 10.

   _____ 7, 9, 9, 11, 14 _____

3. There are 7 whole numbers in a group. The greatest number is 20 and the least is 8. The median is 12 and the mode is 12. The mean is 13.

   _____ 8, 10, 12, 12, 14, 15, 20 _____

4. There are 7 whole numbers in a group. The least number is 5 and the greatest is 15. The mean and the median are 11. The mode is 15.

   _____ 5, 7, 9, 11, 15, 15, 15 _____

5. There are 7 whole numbers in a group. The least number is 11 and the greatest is 17. The mean and the median are 14. There is no mode.

   _____ 11, 12, 13, 14, 15, 16, 17 _____

6. There are 7 whole numbers in a group. The least number is 15 and the greatest is 33. The mean is 23. The median is 22. The mode is 19.

   _____ 15, 19, 19, 22, 25, 28, 33 _____

7. There are 7 whole numbers in a group. The greatest number is 37 and the least is 21. The median is 29. The mean is 28. The mode is 31.

   _____ 21, 23, 24, 29, 31, 31, 37 _____

Name _____

Draw Your Own Conclusions

Conduct a survey. Ask your classmates to name their favorite hobbies.

1. Record your data in the table at the right.
   Possible answers are given.

FAVORITE HOBBIES	
Hobby	**Number of Students**
Sports	12
Reading	5
Video games	7
Collections	3
Other	4

2. Make a bar graph or a circle graph of the data in your table. A bar graph of the "Favorite Hobbies" data is shown at the right.

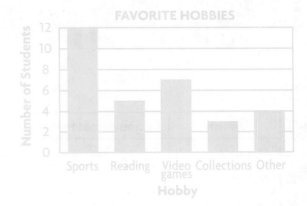

FAVORITE HOBBIES

Compare your graph with this graph about favorite hobbies from Memphis Middle School students.
Possible answers are given.

3. Which hobbies do both groups of students enjoy?

   _____ reading and collections _____

4. Which hobby was the favorite hobby of the Memphis students? of your classmates?

   _____ reading; sports _____

5. Are there any major differences between the favorite hobbies selected by the Memphis students and your classmates? Explain.

   _____ Sports is the major hobby of my friends, but it wasn't _____

   _____ even mentioned in the other survey. _____

© Harcourt

FAVORITE HOBBIES (5 YEARS AGO)

Building models
Stamp collection
Other
Coin collection
Reading
Crafts
Trading cards

Using Graphs

The bar graph gives an estimate of the number of calories burned per hour for different activities. However, the names of the activities were left off the graph. Use the clues below to complete the table.

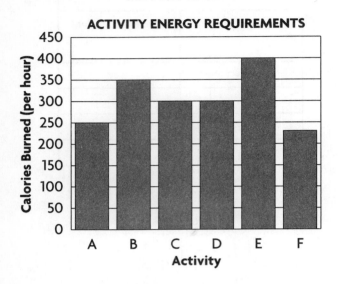

ACTIVITY ENERGY REQUIREMENTS

	Activity	Calories Burned Per Hour
1.	Aerobics	300
2.	Walking	300
3.	Canoeing	230
4.	Roller skating	350
5.	Lawn mowing	250
6.	Chopping wood	400

CLUES

- Chopping wood for an hour burns 170 calories more than paddling a canoe for an hour.
- If you walk for 30 minutes, you will burn 25 calories more than if you spend 30 minutes mowing the yard.
- Walking and aerobics burn the same number of calories per hour.
- Roller skating burns more calories than walking but fewer than chopping wood.

7. Walking for 20 minutes burns the same number of calories as 15 minutes spent participating in which activity?

chopping wood
_____

Divided-Bar Graphs

In a divided-bar graph, each bar can show more than one piece of data.

During the twentieth century, the American population changed from mostly rural to mostly urban. People moved from farms or small villages to larger cities. The table and divided-bar graph show this change for selected years from 1910 through 1990.

Year	Urban Population	Rural Population
1910	46%	54%
1930	56%	44%
1950	64%	36%
1970	74%	26%
1990	75%	25%

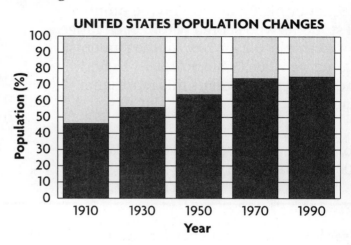

1. The data in the table and graph show that the population gradually became more urban. Which color in each bar represents the percent of the population that was living in cities? How do you know?

   Possible answer: Dark grey represents the urban

   population because the height of that part of the bars

   increases over the years.

2. In which year was the population most evenly divided between urban and rural? How does the graph show this?

   Possible answer: 1910; in that year the 2 parts of the bar

   are closest to being equal in length.

3. Between which two pairs of years was the movement of the population the greatest?

   between 1910 and 1930 and between 1950 and 1970

4. If the trend continued, what percent of the population would you expect to be urban in the 2000 census? Explain your reasoning.

   Possible answer: About 76% or 77%; the rate of change

   has slowed greatly, and there are fewer people left in

   rural areas to move to cities.

Name _____

A Relative Frequency Histogram

Mrs. Sutton graded her students' history tests and posted the grades in the form of a relative frequency histogram.

There are 25 students in Mrs. Sutton's history class. You can use the relative frequency histogram to find the number of students who scored within each range. For example, 0.2, or 20%, of the students scored between 91% and 100%. To find the number of students this represents, multiply:

$$0.2 \times 25 = 5$$

So, 5 students scored between 91% and 100% on the history test.

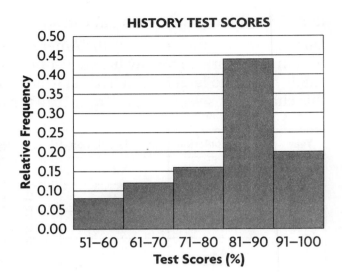

HISTORY TEST SCORES

Use the relative frequency histogram to find the number of students who scored in each of the other ranges. Complete the chart. Then answer the questions.

1.

Test Score Range (%)	Number of Students
91–100	5
81–90	11
71–80	4
61–70	3
51–60	2

2. How many students scored at least 81% on the test?

_____ 16 students _____

3. Can you calculate the mean score for the test? Explain why or why not.

_____ Possible answer: No; you cannot calculate the mean _____

_____ because the actual scores are not given, just the _____

_____ numbers of scores within specific ranges. _____

© Harcourt

CW30   Challenge

Name _____

Name the Amount!

Write your answer.

1. Sue received scores of 79, 83, 76, and 100 on her first four math tests. What score must she get on her fifth test to have an average of 85 for all five tests?

_____87_____

2. Kyle bowled scores of 112, 126, 98, and 118 in his first four games. What score must he bowl in his fifth game to have an average of 120 for all five games?

_____146_____

3. In his first five rounds of golf, Jon scored 84, 71, 77, 68, and 74. What score must Jon achieve in his sixth round in order to have an average of 75 for all six rounds?

_____76_____

4. Matt scored 89, 93, 100, 77, and 81 on his first five science tests. What score must he earn on his sixth test in order to have an average of 90 for all six tests?

_____100_____

5. In her first five games, Betty bowled 128, 116, 104, 112, and 134. What must she bowl in her sixth game in order to have an average of 120 for all six games?

_____126_____

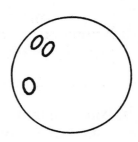

6. The following numbers of moviegoers saw the first six showings of a recently released movie: 213, 322, 278, 309, 258, 296. How many movie fans must attend the seventh showing in order to have an average of 280 people per showing?

_____284 people_____

7. The following numbers of students went to the first five basketball games: 180, 200, 175, 200, 205. How many students must attend the sixth game in order to have an average of 200 students per game?

_____240 students_____

Challenge CW31

Name _____

Scale the Heights

For each set of data, assume that you are going to draw a bar graph.
Describe the scale you would use for the vertical axis. Include the minimum
value, the maximum value, and the size of each interval. Possible answers are given.

1. Maximum animal speeds: zebra, 40 mi per hr; lion, 50 mi per hr;
   grizzly bear, 30 mi per hr; elephant, 25 mi per hr

   minimum: 0; maximum: 50; interval size: 10

2. Average animal life spans: horse, 20 years; leopard, 12 years; Asian
   elephant, 40 years; rabbit, 5 years

   minimum: 0; maximum: 50; interval size: 5

3. Countries with the fewest people: Nauru, 10,605; Palau, 18,467; San
   Marino, 25,061; Tuvalu, 10,588

   minimum: 0; maximum: 30,000; interval size: 5,000

4. Professional basketball games won during the 1998–1999 season:
   Miami Heat, 33; New Jersey Nets, 16; Orlando Magic, 33;
   Philadelphia 76ers, 28; Washington Wizards, 18

   minimum: 0; maximum: 35; interval size: 5

5. Miles of border shared with the United States: Mexico, 1,933 mi;
   Pacific Ocean, 7,623 mi; Atlantic Ocean, 2,069 mi; Gulf of Mexico,
   1,631 mi

   minimum: 0; maximum: 8,000; interval size: 1,000

6. Number of members of the U.S. House of Representatives:
   New York, 31; California, 52; Rhode Island, 2; Florida, 23

   minimum: 0; maximum: 60; interval size: 4

7. Warmest temperatures ever recorded, by continent: Africa, 136°F;
   Asia, 129°F; North America, 134°F; Antarctica, 59°F

   minimum: 0; maximum: 140; interval size: 10

8. Highest point on the continent: North America, 20,320 ft; Australia,
   7,310 ft, Asia, 29,035 ft; Europe, 18,510 ft; South America, 22,834 ft

   minimum: 0; maximum: 30,000; interval size: 2,000

9. Most widely used languages in the world (in millions of speakers):
   Mandarin, 1,075; English, 514; Hindi, 496

   minimum: 0; maximum: 1,200; interval size: 100

© Harcourt

Name _____

Divisible or Not

Each statement below about divisibility is given as a rule. If you think the rule is correct, write *Correct* and give an explanation of why it is true. If you think the rule is incorrect, write *Incorrect* and give a counterexample. A counterexample is an example that shows the rule is not true for every possibility. Possible explanations and counterexamples are given.

1. Every number that is divisible by 4 is also divisible by 2.

   Correct; if a number is divisible by 4, it must be an even number, and all even numbers are divisible by 2.

2. If a number is divisible by 6, then it is also divisible by 3.

   Correct; part of the rule for divisibility by 6 is that a number be divisible by 3.

3. All numbers that are divisible by 2 are also divisible by 4.

   Incorrect; counterexamples include 6, 10, 14, and 18.

4. All numbers divisible by 5 are divisible by 2.

   Incorrect; counterexamples include 5, 15, 25, and 35.

5. If a number is divisible by 9, then it is also divisible by 3.

   Correct; the sum of the digits of any number divisible by 9 will be a number that is also divisible by 3.

6. All numbers divisible by 2 and 4 are also divisible by 8.

   Incorrect; counterexamples include 4, 12, 20, and 28.

7. If the last digit of a number is 0, the number is not divisible by 9.

   Incorrect; counterexamples include 90, 180, 270, and 360.

© Harcourt

Name _____

Prime Patterns

When you divide prime numbers by certain single-digit numbers, some interesting patterns occur. Complete the tables below to discover them.

Prime Number	17	29	37	43	59	61	67	79	83	97
Remainder when divided by 3	2	2	1	1	2	1	1	1	2	1

1. What pattern do you see in the remainders when prime numbers are divided by 3?

   _____Possible answer: The remainder is either 1 or 2._____

2. Choose 3 three-digit prime numbers. Divide by 3. Check the pattern. Answers will vary.

   prime number: _____ _____ _____

   remainder: _____ _____ _____

Prime Number	17	29	37	43	59	61	67	79	83	97
Remainder when divided by 4	1	1	1	3	3	1	3	3	3	1

3. What pattern do you see in the remainders when prime numbers are divided by 4?

   _____Possible answer: The remainder is either 1 or 3._____

4. Choose 3 three-digit prime numbers. Divide by 4. Check the pattern. Answers will vary.

   prime number: _____ _____ _____

   remainder: _____ _____ _____

Prime Number	17	29	37	43	59	61	67	79	83	97
Remainder when divided by 6	5	5	1	1	5	1	1	1	5	1

5. What pattern do you see in the remainders when prime numbers are divided by 6?

   _____Possible answer: The remainder is either 1 or 5._____

6. Choose 3 three-digit prime numbers. Divide by 6. Check the pattern. Answers will vary.

   prime number: _____ _____ _____

   remainder: _____ _____ _____

Name _____

Figure the Prime Factors

Shade one box in each row to show the prime factors of the given number.

1. 84

7	2
2	3
11	2
2	5

2. 225

5	3
5	2
3	7
2	3

3. 56

2	7
2	3
5	2
3	2

4. 144

7	3
3	5
3	2
11	2
2	5
2	7

5. 234

3	13
7	3
2	3
5	2

6. 96

5	3
2	11
2	5
7	2
2	3
2	5

7. 208

13	2
11	2
2	5
2	3
2	5

8. 340

17	13
5	7
3	2
2	11

9. 456

17	19
11	3
7	2
3	2
2	5

Multiple Relationships

Fill in each blank with a number from the box below. Then, identify the relationship described. The first two are done for you. You will not use every number in the box.

108	62	~~42~~	8	~~51~~	19	120	36
180	95	9	15	16	310	192	25
75	30	94	60	27	64	~~12~~	35

1. 17 is to __51__ and 85 as 19 is to 57 and 95. What is the relationship?
   _____ 17 is the GCF of 51 and 85; 19 is the GCF of 57 and 95. _____

2. __42__ is to 6 and 14 as 48 is to __12__ and 16. What is the relationship?
   _____ 42 is the LCM of 6 and 14; 48 is the LCM of 12 and 16. _____

3. 45 is to __9__ and 15 as 120 is to 24 and 30. What is the relationship?
   _____ 45 is the LCM of 9 and 15; 120 is the LCM of 24 and 30. _____

   _____

4. 36 is to 108 and 180 as __64__ is to 192 and 320. What is the relationship?
   _____ 36 is the GCF of 108 and 180; 64 is the GCF of 192 _____

   _____ and 320. _____

5. 47 is to 94 and 235 as 62 is to 124 and __310__. What is the relationship?
   _____ 47 is the GCF of 94 and 235; 62 is the GCF of _____

   _____ 124 and 310. _____

6. 105 is to 15 and 35 as __108__ is to 12 and 27. What is the relationship?
   _____ 105 is the LCM of 15 and 35; 108 is the LCM of _____

   _____ 12 and 27. _____

7. 12 is to 24 and 36 as __25__ is to 50 and 75. What is the relationship?
   _____ 12 is the GCF of 24 and 36; 25 is the GCF of 50 and 75. _____

   _____

Name _____

Organization is the Key!

Solve each problem by making an organized list of the data.

1. Ana and Juan are going shopping for gifts. They need to go to a toy store (T), a stationery store (S), and a jewelry store (J). Make a list of all the possible orders in which they can visit the stores. How many choices do they have for the order in which they visit the stores?

   S-T-J; S-J-T; J-S-T; J-T-S; T-J-S; T-S-J; 6 choices

2. Suppose Ana needs to stop at her bank before going to any stores. In how many different orders can they make their four stops?

   6 different orders

3. Assume it does not matter whether Ana goes to the bank before shopping or after shopping. In how many different orders can they then make their four stops?

   12 different orders

4. Juan and his three friends, Amy, Vijay, and Yoko, will each talk to one another on the phone today before agreeing where to meet after he finishes shopping. If each friend speaks to the others once, how many phone calls will there be in all? (Keep in mind that once Juan calls Amy, for example, there is no need for Amy to call Juan.)

   6 phone calls

5. When wrapping three gifts, Ana has a choice of three different wrapping papers: one with stripes, one with balloons, and one with elephants. She cannot decide whether to wrap all the gifts in the same paper or to use a different paper for each gift. In how many different ways can she wrap the three gifts? (Count each combination of wrapping papers only once.) List the ways.

   10 ways

   SSS, SSB, SSE, BBB, BBS, BBE, EEE, EES, EEB, SEB

6. If Ana decides to use a different wrapping paper for each gift, in how many different ways can she wrap her three gifts?

   6 ways

© Harcourt

Name _____

Fraction Flowers

Shade each petal that contains a fraction in simplest form.
Then write the other fractions in simplest form.

1.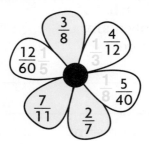

2.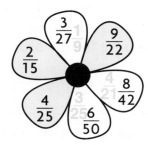

3.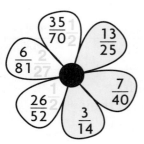

4.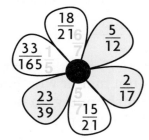

5.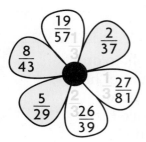

6.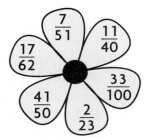

7.

8.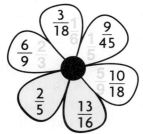

9.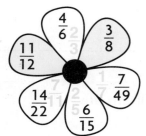

10.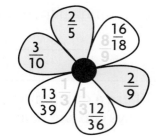

Name _____

Fraction Squares

Shade the squares that show fractions equivalent to the mixed number in the center.

1.

$\frac{93}{31}$	$\frac{41}{6}$	$\frac{30}{12}$
$\frac{35}{14}$	$2\frac{1}{2}$	$\frac{20}{12}$
$\frac{65}{26}$	$\frac{37}{13}$	$\frac{10}{4}$

2.

$\frac{24}{7}$	$\frac{143}{39}$	$\frac{121}{33}$
$\frac{45}{14}$	$3\frac{2}{3}$	$\frac{110}{30}$
$\frac{66}{18}$	$\frac{95}{26}$	$\frac{36}{12}$

3.

$\frac{242}{55}$	$\frac{18}{4}$	$\frac{21}{5}$
$\frac{286}{65}$	$4\frac{2}{5}$	$\frac{250}{75}$
$\frac{168}{32}$	$\frac{154}{35}$	$\frac{220}{50}$

4.

$\frac{96}{18}$	$\frac{336}{64}$	$\frac{126}{14}$
$\frac{105}{20}$	$5\frac{1}{4}$	$\frac{63}{12}$
$\frac{252}{48}$	$\frac{210}{40}$	$\frac{122}{24}$

5.

$\frac{340}{50}$	$\frac{98}{13}$	$\frac{220}{33}$
$\frac{140}{21}$	$6\frac{2}{3}$	$\frac{160}{32}$
$\frac{320}{48}$	$\frac{100}{15}$	$\frac{450}{45}$

6.

$\frac{105}{10}$	$\frac{17}{3}$	$\frac{43}{4}$
$\frac{42}{4}$	$10\frac{1}{2}$	$\frac{872}{119}$
$\frac{420}{40}$	$\frac{84}{8}$	$\frac{273}{26}$

Challenge CW39

Name _____

Let's Compare

For each exercise, choose a
fraction from the box at the right.

$$\frac{19}{24}, \quad \frac{7}{24}, \quad \frac{7}{10}, \quad \frac{1}{2}$$

1. Carl, Philip, and Monica were discussing how they had spent last summer. Carl said that he stayed at his grandmother's house for half the summer. Philip said he stayed at his aunt's house for $\frac{2}{3}$ of the summer. Monica said she was away for a greater fraction of the summer than either of the two boys. If she was away for less than $\frac{3}{4}$ of the summer, what fraction of the summer was she away?

_____ $\frac{7}{10}$ of the summer _____

2. When her cat had kittens, Mrs. Banks gave three of them to neighbors while they were still very small. The one she gave to Elise weighed $\frac{2}{3}$ lb. The one that Carmela received weighed $\frac{3}{8}$ lb. The kitten that Denise took home weighed more than Carmela's kitten, but less than Elise's. What fraction of a pound did Denise's kitten weigh?

_____ $\frac{1}{2}$ lb _____

3. Each morning, Maria rides her bike $\frac{1}{3}$ mi to school. Angela walks the $\frac{1}{4}$ mi between her home and school. James skateboards from home to school, a distance less than Maria rides, but more than Angela walks. What fraction of a mile does James skateboard to school?

_____ $\frac{7}{24}$ mi _____

4. Sandra, Jackson, and Shari all have the same size box of markers. Sandra still has $\frac{5}{6}$ of all the markers that were originally in her box. Jackson has $\frac{3}{4}$ of the original number. Shari has more markers than one of her friends, but less than the other. What fraction of the original number of markers does Shari still have?

_____ $\frac{19}{24}$ of the markers _____

CW40   Challenge

Decimal Patterns

Find the next three terms in the pattern. Then write the rule for the pattern.

1. $\frac{1}{5}$, $\frac{2}{5}$, $\frac{3}{5}$, $\frac{4}{5}$, $\frac{5}{5}$, $\frac{6}{5}$, $\frac{7}{5}$, $\frac{8}{5}$, $\frac{9}{5}$
    ↓   ↓   ↓   ↓   ↓   ↓   ↓   ↓   ↓

    0.20   0.40   0.60   0.80   1.00   1.20   _1.40_ _1.60_ _1.80_

    Add $\frac{1}{5}$ (0.20) to previous number.

Rule: _____

2. $\frac{11}{2}$, $\frac{10}{2}$, $\frac{9}{2}$, $\frac{8}{2}$, $\frac{7}{2}$, $\frac{6}{2}$, $\frac{5}{2}$, $\frac{4}{2}$, $\frac{3}{2}$
    ↓   ↓   ↓   ↓   ↓   ↓   ↓   ↓   ↓

    5.5   5.0   4.5   4.0   3.5   3.0   _2.5_   _2.0_   _1.5_

    Subtract $\frac{1}{2}$ (0.5) from previous number.

Rule: _____

3. $\frac{3}{10}$, $\frac{6}{10}$, $\frac{9}{10}$, $\frac{12}{10}$, $\frac{15}{10}$, $\frac{18}{10}$, $\frac{21}{10}$, $\frac{24}{10}$, $\frac{27}{10}$
    ↓   ↓   ↓   ↓   ↓   ↓   ↓   ↓   ↓

    0.3   0.6   0.9   1.2   1.5   1.8   _2.1_   _2.4_   _2.7_

    Add $\frac{3}{10}$ (0.3) to previous number.

Rule: _____

4. $\frac{25}{4}$, $\frac{24}{4}$, $\frac{23}{4}$, $\frac{22}{4}$, $\frac{21}{4}$, $\frac{20}{4}$, $\frac{19}{4}$, $\frac{18}{4}$, $\frac{17}{4}$
    ↓   ↓   ↓   ↓   ↓   ↓   ↓   ↓   ↓

    6.25   6.00   5.75   5.50   5.25   5.00   _4.75_ _4.50_ _4.25_

    Subtract $\frac{1}{4}$ (0.25) from previous number.

Rule: _____

5. $\frac{44}{10}$, $\frac{40}{10}$, $\frac{36}{10}$, $\frac{32}{10}$, $\frac{28}{10}$, $\frac{24}{10}$, $\frac{20}{10}$, $\frac{16}{10}$, $\frac{12}{10}$, $\frac{8}{10}$
    ↓   ↓   ↓   ↓   ↓   ↓   ↓   ↓   ↓   ↓

    4.4   4.0   3.6   3.2   2.8   2.4   2.0   _1.6_   _1.2_   _0.8_

    Subtract $\frac{4}{10}$ (0.4) from previous number.

Rule: _____

6. $\frac{99}{100}$, $\frac{88}{100}$, $\frac{77}{100}$, $\frac{66}{100}$, $\frac{55}{100}$, $\frac{44}{100}$, $\frac{33}{100}$, $\frac{22}{100}$
    ↓   ↓   ↓   ↓   ↓   ↓   ↓   ↓

    0.99   0.88   0.77   0.66   0.55   _0.44_ _0.33_ _0.22_

    Subtract $\frac{11}{100}$ (0.11) from previous number.

Rule: _____

You Write the Problem

An error was made when this book was created. Somehow, the answers to the problems on this page were printed, but the problems were omitted. Help the printer out by creating an estimation problem for each answer below. Make sure your problems involve fractions. Problems will vary.

1. _____

_____

_____

_____

_____

_____

Answer — about $3\frac{1}{2}$ mi

2. _____

_____

_____

_____

_____

_____

Answer — about 4 yd of fabric

3. _____

_____

_____

_____

_____

_____

Answer — about 15 ft of wire

4. _____

_____

_____

_____

_____

_____

Answer — about 3 c of flour

5. _____

_____

_____

_____

_____

_____

Answer — about $7\frac{1}{2}$ yd of ribbon

6. _____

_____

_____

_____

_____

_____

Answer — about 4 hr

7. _____

_____

_____

_____

_____

_____

Answer — about 12 gal

8. _____

_____

_____

_____

_____

_____

Answer — about $5\frac{1}{2}$ in.

Name _____

Sum It Up

The shaded portion of each figure below models a fraction. Use the figures to find each sum. Write your answer in simplest form.

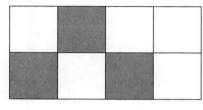

A

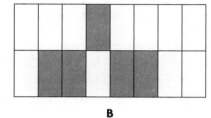

B

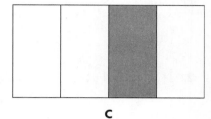

C

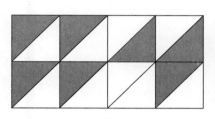

D

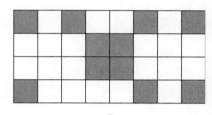

E

F

1. A + C = _____ $\frac{5}{8}$

2. F − B = _____ $\frac{1}{32}$

3. E − D = _____ $\frac{1}{16}$

4. C + F = _____ $\frac{19}{32}$

5. A + B = _____ $\frac{11}{16}$

6. E − C = _____ $\frac{1}{4}$

7. B + D = _____ $\frac{3}{4}$

8. A + F = _____ $\frac{23}{32}$

9. D − A = _____ $\frac{1}{16}$

10. C + B = _____ $\frac{9}{16}$

11. E + A = _____ $\frac{7}{8}$

12. D − F = _____ $\frac{3}{32}$

13. C + D = _____ $\frac{11}{16}$

14. E − B + C = _____ $\frac{7}{16}$

15. F + A − D = _____ $\frac{9}{32}$

16. A − B + C = _____ $\frac{5}{16}$

17. E − F + D = _____ $\frac{19}{32}$

18. A + F − B = _____ $\frac{13}{32}$

Name _____

Addition Patterns

Write the next three terms. Then identify the rule.

1. 10; $14\frac{1}{5}$; $18\frac{2}{5}$; $22\frac{3}{5}$; ___$26\frac{4}{5}$___; ___31___; ___$35\frac{1}{5}$___

   Rule: ___Add $4\frac{1}{5}$ to previous term.___

2. 1; $2\frac{1}{4}$; $3\frac{1}{2}$; $4\frac{3}{4}$; ___6___; ___$7\frac{1}{4}$___; ___$8\frac{1}{2}$___

   Rule: ___Add $1\frac{1}{4}$ to previous term.___

3. 5; $7\frac{1}{5}$; $9\frac{2}{5}$; $11\frac{3}{5}$; ___$13\frac{4}{5}$___; ___16___; ___$18\frac{1}{5}$___

   Rule: ___Add $2\frac{1}{5}$ to previous term.___

4. 1; $2\frac{3}{8}$; $3\frac{3}{4}$; $5\frac{1}{8}$; ___$6\frac{1}{2}$___; ___$7\frac{7}{8}$___; ___$9\frac{1}{4}$___

   Rule: ___Add $1\frac{3}{8}$ to previous term.___

5. 4; $7\frac{2}{9}$; $10\frac{4}{9}$; $13\frac{2}{3}$; ___$16\frac{8}{9}$___; ___$20\frac{1}{9}$___; ___$23\frac{1}{3}$___

   Rule: ___Add $3\frac{2}{9}$ to previous term.___

6. 2; $4\frac{3}{10}$; $6\frac{3}{5}$; $8\frac{9}{10}$; ___$11\frac{1}{5}$___; ___$13\frac{1}{2}$___; ___$15\frac{4}{5}$___

   Rule: ___Add $2\frac{3}{10}$ to previous term.___

7. 3; $4\frac{1}{3}$; $5\frac{2}{3}$; 7; ___$8\frac{1}{3}$___; ___$9\frac{2}{3}$___; ___11___

   Rule: ___Add $1\frac{1}{3}$ to previous term.___

8. 1; $3\frac{1}{6}$; $5\frac{1}{3}$; $7\frac{1}{2}$; ___$9\frac{2}{3}$___; ___$11\frac{5}{6}$___; ___14___

   Rule: ___Add $2\frac{1}{6}$ to previous term.___

9. 8; $9\frac{1}{8}$; $10\frac{1}{4}$; $11\frac{3}{8}$; ___$12\frac{1}{2}$___; ___$13\frac{5}{8}$___; ___$14\frac{3}{4}$___

   Rule: ___Add $1\frac{1}{8}$ to previous term.___

10. 12; $14\frac{3}{4}$; $17\frac{1}{2}$; $20\frac{1}{4}$; ___23___; ___$25\frac{3}{4}$___; ___$28\frac{1}{2}$___

    Rule: ___Add $2\frac{3}{4}$ to previous term.___

Puzzling Fractions

Match each exercise in Column 1 with its sum or difference in Column 2. Then, to discover the Math Tip in the box, write each corresponding letter above the line marked with the exercise number.

Column 1	Letter		Column 2
1. $2\frac{1}{3} - 1\frac{3}{4}$	H		A. $1\frac{8}{9}$
2. $5\frac{1}{2} - 3\frac{1}{4}$	O		B. $3\frac{7}{12}$
3. $4\frac{7}{9} - 2\frac{8}{9}$	A		D. $2\frac{5}{6}$
4. $6\frac{2}{3} - 5\frac{1}{3}$	S		E. $2\frac{1}{8}$
5. $4\frac{2}{3} - 1\frac{5}{6}$	D		F. $2\frac{1}{20}$
6. $5\frac{3}{10} - 1\frac{4}{5}$	L		H. $\frac{7}{12}$
7. $5\frac{1}{6} - 2\frac{2}{3}$	U		I. $6\frac{7}{12}$
8. $6\frac{3}{4} - 3\frac{1}{6}$	B		L. $3\frac{1}{2}$
9. $2\frac{1}{5} - 1\frac{1}{7}$	N		M. $6\frac{8}{15}$
10. $7\frac{11}{12} - 5\frac{1}{6}$	W		N. $1\frac{2}{35}$
11. $3\frac{3}{8} - 1\frac{1}{4}$	E		O. $2\frac{1}{4}$
12. $6\frac{2}{5} - 1\frac{7}{20}$	P		P. $5\frac{1}{20}$
13. $8\frac{5}{12} - 1\frac{5}{6}$	I		R. $\frac{8}{9}$
14. $5\frac{2}{7} - 1\frac{1}{3}$	T		S. $1\frac{1}{3}$
15. $9\frac{2}{3} - 3\frac{2}{15}$	M		T. $3\frac{20}{21}$
16. $4\frac{7}{10} - 2\frac{13}{20}$	F		U. $2\frac{1}{2}$
17. $4\frac{2}{9} - 3\frac{1}{3}$	R		W. $2\frac{3}{4}$

Math Tip

A	N	S	W	E	R	S		S	H	O	U	L	D	
3	9	4	10	11	17	4		4	1	2	7	6	5	

B	E		I	N	
8	11		13	9	

S	I	M	P	L	E	S	T		F	O	R	M	!
4	13	15	12	6	11	4	14		16	2	17	15	

Name _____

Pyramid Patterns in a Diagram

Pascal's Triangle is an arrangement of numbers that has been used for many years to solve problems. It was named for a French mathematician who may have discovered it.

```
                    1                        Row 0
                 1     1                     Row 1
              1     2     1                  Row 2
           1     3     3     1               Row 3
        1     4     6     4     1            Row 4
     1     5    10    10     5     1         Row 5
```

Use Pascal's Triangle to answer the following questions.

1. Find each group of numbers in the diagram.

```
    1    2          3    1          3    3          4    6
       3               4               6              10
```

From these groups, can you describe the pattern that is used to create the triangle?

The bottom number is the sum of the two numbers above it.

2. The next row of the triangle contains these numbers.

    1   __6__   15   20   __15__   6   1

Use the pattern to fill in the missing numbers.

3. A section further down the triangle contains the following numbers.

    1   7   21   35   35   21   7   1

    1   __8__   28   __56__   70   __56__   __28__   8   1

Use the pattern to fill in the missing numbers.

4. When you add the numbers in the rows, an interesting pattern develops. Add the numbers in rows 0 through 5. Describe what you find.

The sums of the rows are the powers of 2.

5. What will the sum be for row 6? row 7? _____ 64, 128 _____

6. Find the diagonals that represent the first 5 counting numbers (1, 2, 3, 4, and 5). If the pattern is extended, in which row will the eighth counting number be found?

row 8

© Harcourt

CW46 Challenge

Estimation Sense

If you estimate without thinking about the situation, you can get results that simply do not make any sense. Such errors can lead to other more serious errors. Possible answers are given.

Solve.

1. Mr. Axel won $7,328,493 in the state lottery. He promised to give $\frac{1}{10}$ of the money to several charities and keep the rest for himself. He rounded $\frac{1}{10}$ to 0, and then multiplied to see that each charity would get $0! What is wrong with Mr. Axel's approach to this problem? What might he do to get a more accurate estimate?

$\frac{1}{10}$ of such a large amount of money is a lot more than $0.

Mr. Axel might remember that multiplying by $\frac{1}{10}$ is the

same as dividing by 10 or multiplying by 0.1.

2. The Martin family started a savings account with $1,000 that grew at the same rate every year. There was always $1\frac{1}{8}$ times as much money at the end of each year than at the beginning of the year. The Martins rounded the growth rate of $1\frac{1}{8}$ times to 1, and estimated how much they would have in 10 years. What was their estimated total? What is wrong with their approach to this problem?

The Martins' estimation showed that they would end up

with $1,000, because they were always multiplying by 1.

They should have realized that rounding to 1 can create

inaccuracies when repeated multiplications are being

performed.

3. Think about the situations in Problems 1 and 2 above. What would you say to someone who estimates by rounding small fractions to 0 and fractions near 1 to 1?

I might warn them to use common sense when

applying rounding rules so that they don't make a

mistake. They should ask, "Does my estimate make

sense in this situation?"

Name _____

Fraction Flowers

Color the petals containing factors of the product in the circle. Remember to use GCFs to simplify the factors before multiplying!

1.

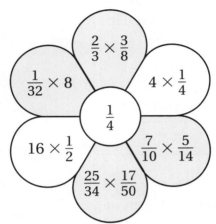

2.

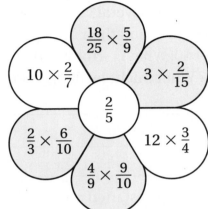

3.

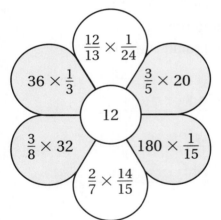

4.

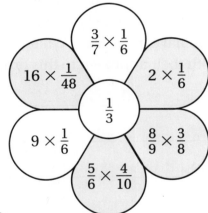

5.

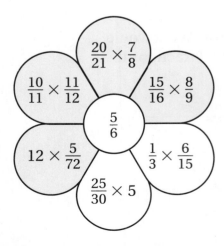

6.

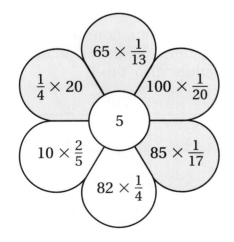

CW48 Challenge

Fraction Analogies

Read each analogy. Explain how each pair of numbers is related.
The first one is done for you.

1. $2\frac{1}{3}$ is to $3\frac{1}{2}$ as $4\frac{3}{8}$ is to $6\frac{9}{16}$.

Think: What number times $2\frac{1}{3}$ equals $3\frac{1}{2}$?

$3\frac{1}{2}$ is the product of $2\frac{1}{3}$ and $1\frac{1}{2}$, just as $6\frac{9}{16}$ is the product of $4\frac{3}{8}$ and $1\frac{1}{2}$.

2. $1\frac{2}{5}$ is to $2\frac{9}{20}$ as $3\frac{1}{2}$ is to $6\frac{1}{8}$.

$2\frac{9}{20}$ is the product of $1\frac{2}{5}$ and $1\frac{3}{4}$,

as $6\frac{1}{8}$ is the product of $3\frac{1}{2}$ and $1\frac{3}{4}$.

3. $4\frac{3}{8}$ is to $1\frac{3}{32}$ as $5\frac{3}{4}$ is to $1\frac{7}{16}$.

$1\frac{3}{32}$ is the product of $4\frac{3}{8}$ and $\frac{1}{4}$, as $1\frac{7}{16}$ is the product of

$5\frac{3}{4}$ and $\frac{1}{4}$.

4. $3\frac{4}{5}$ is to $9\frac{1}{2}$ as $4\frac{7}{8}$ is to $12\frac{3}{16}$.

$9\frac{1}{2}$ is the product of $3\frac{4}{5}$ and $2\frac{1}{2}$, as $12\frac{3}{16}$ is the product of

$4\frac{7}{8}$ and $2\frac{1}{2}$.

5. $5\frac{1}{3}$ is to $1\frac{1}{15}$ as $6\frac{3}{4}$ is to $1\frac{7}{20}$.

$1\frac{1}{15}$ is the product of $5\frac{1}{3}$ and $\frac{1}{5}$, as $1\frac{7}{20}$ is the product of

$6\frac{3}{4}$ and $\frac{1}{5}$.

6. $9\frac{5}{6}$ is to $11\frac{1}{16}$ as $3\frac{1}{4}$ is to $3\frac{21}{32}$.

$11\frac{1}{16}$ is the product of $9\frac{5}{6}$ and $1\frac{1}{8}$, as $3\frac{21}{32}$ is the product

of $3\frac{1}{4}$ and $1\frac{1}{8}$.

7. $2\frac{5}{12}$ is to $3\frac{2}{9}$ as $4\frac{5}{6}$ is to $6\frac{4}{9}$.

$3\frac{2}{9}$ is the product of $2\frac{5}{12}$ and $1\frac{1}{3}$, as $6\frac{4}{9}$ is the product of

$4\frac{5}{6}$ and $1\frac{1}{3}$.

Name _____

Divide to Find a Message

Match each exercise in Column 1 with its quotient in Column 2.
Then write each corresponding letter on the line below marked
with the exercise number to discover the Math Tip.

Column 1

1. $\frac{3}{4} \div \frac{1}{2}$ _____L_____

2. $6 \div \frac{1}{9}$ _____Q_____

3. $\frac{8}{11} \div \frac{1}{3}$ _____G_____

4. $10 \div \frac{2}{5}$ _____A_____

5. $\frac{11}{12} \div \frac{1}{3}$ _____N_____

6. $\frac{1}{10} \div 5$ _____C_____

7. $\frac{3}{4} \div \frac{1}{8}$ _____T_____

8. $\frac{5}{7} \div 10$ _____X_____

9. $\frac{4}{5} \div \frac{2}{10}$ _____Z_____

10. $3 \div \frac{2}{9}$ _____E_____

11. $8 \div \frac{3}{8}$ _____V_____

12. $\frac{7}{8} \div \frac{1}{2}$ _____B_____

13. $\frac{1}{2} \div 2$ _____S_____

14. $12 \div \frac{1}{6}$ _____U_____

15. $\frac{2}{7} \div \frac{1}{8}$ _____P_____

16. $18 \div \frac{2}{3}$ _____J_____

17. $\frac{3}{20} \div \frac{3}{10}$ _____I_____

18. $15 \div \frac{1}{3}$ _____W_____

19. $\frac{3}{5} \div \frac{1}{3}$ _____R_____

20. $11 \div \frac{1}{2}$ _____D_____

21. $\frac{5}{7} \div \frac{10}{14}$ _____F_____

22. $\frac{2}{3} \div \frac{8}{9}$ _____Y_____

23. $5 \div \frac{1}{15}$ _____H_____

24. $\frac{7}{8} \div \frac{1}{4}$ _____O_____

25. $10 \div \frac{1}{5}$ _____K_____

26. $\frac{5}{8} \div \frac{1}{3}$ _____M_____

Column 2

A. 25

B. $1\frac{3}{4}$

C. $\frac{1}{50}$

D. 22

E. $13\frac{1}{2}$

F. 1

G. $2\frac{2}{11}$

H. 75

I. $\frac{1}{2}$

J. 27

K. 50

L. $1\frac{1}{2}$

M. $1\frac{7}{8}$

N. $2\frac{3}{4}$

O. $3\frac{1}{2}$

P. $2\frac{2}{7}$

Q. 54

R. $1\frac{4}{5}$

S. $\frac{1}{4}$

T. 6

U. 72

V. $21\frac{1}{3}$

W. 45

X. $\frac{1}{14}$

Y. $\frac{3}{4}$

Z. 4

M T H E   P R O D U C T
  7   23   10   15   19   24   20   14   6   7

A

T O F   A   N U M B E R
  24   21   4   5   14   26   12   10   19

H A N D   I T S
  4   5   20   17   7   13

T

I R E C I P R O C A L
  19   10   6   17   15   19   24   6   4   1

P I S   O N E .
  17   13   24   5   10

CW50 Challenge

ABCD Methods

Ann, Badri, Cristina, and Devon measured a redwood deck to determine its area. They made the following sketch to record their measurement. Measurements are in yards.

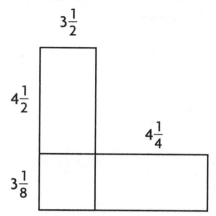

Here's how each of them calculated the area of the deck. Perform each calculation.

1. Ann:

$$4\frac{1}{2} \times 3\frac{1}{2} + 3\frac{1}{8} \times 3\frac{1}{2} + 4\frac{1}{4} \times 3\frac{1}{8} = \underline{\quad 39\frac{31}{32} \quad}$$

2. Badri:

$$3\frac{1}{2} \times (4\frac{1}{2} + 3\frac{1}{8}) + 4\frac{1}{4} \times 3\frac{1}{8} = \underline{\quad 39\frac{31}{32} \quad}$$

3. Cristina:

$$4\frac{1}{2} \times 3\frac{1}{2} + 3\frac{1}{8} \times (3\frac{1}{2} + 4\frac{1}{4}) = \underline{\quad 39\frac{31}{32} \quad}$$

4. Devon:

$$(4\frac{1}{2} + 3\frac{1}{8}) \times (3\frac{1}{2} + 4\frac{1}{4}) - (4\frac{1}{2} \times 4\frac{1}{4}) = \underline{\quad 39\frac{31}{32} \quad}$$

5. Who used the correct method? Explain.

The area is $39\frac{31}{32}$ yd². All four of the methods are correct.

Each person chose to do his or her computation in a

different way. Notice that Devon chose to visualize the

deck as a large rectangle with a smaller rectangle

removed.

Venus Versus Earth

Choose a method to complete each problem. Write *paper and pencil,*
mental math, or *calculator.* Possible answers are given for the method.

1. Venus takes 225 Earth days to travel once around the sun.
   About how many trips does it make around the sun during
   2 of our Earth years?

   Answer: _____ 3.25 trips _____

   Method: _____ paper and pencil _____

2. A Venusian year is what percent of an Earth year?

   Answer: _____ 61.6% _____

   Method: _____ calculator _____

3. About how many of Earth's months make a Venusian year?

   Answer: _____ about 7.5 months _____

   Method: _____ mental math _____

4. About how old would you be in Venusian years?

   Answer: __ Possible answer: about 19 years for a 12-year-old __

   Method: _____ calculator _____

5. Imagine that you moved to a space colony on Venus when you
   were 18 years old on Earth. You stayed there for 25 Venusian
   years. About how old would you be then in Earth years? About
   how old in Venusian years?

   Earth years: _____ about 33.5 years old _____

   Venusian years: _____ about 54 years old _____

   Method: _____ paper and pencil _____

6. The diameter of Venus at its equator is 7,520 miles. The diameter
   of Earth at the equator is 7,926 miles. About how much greater is
   Earth's diameter than the diameter of Venus?

   Answer: _____ about 400 miles _____

   Method: _____ mental math _____

Expression Match

Write an algebraic expression for "a number, *a*, less than seven, all divided by 2."

$(7 - a) \div 2$ • The 7 must come first, because *a* is less than 7.
     • To show "all divided by 2," use parentheses.

Draw a line connecting the word expression in Column 1 to the correct algebraic expression in Column 2.

Column 1	Column 2
1. twenty-two less than a number, *a*, all times three	A. $a \div 3 + 22$
2. twenty-two times a number, *a*, plus three	B. $a - 3 + 22$
3. a number, *a*, increased by three, all times twenty-two	C. $22 \times a + 3$
4. a number, *a*, decreased by twenty-two, all divided by three	D. $(a - 22) \times 3$
5. twenty-two times a number, *a*, decreased by three	E. $(22 - a) \times 3$
6. a number, *a*, divided by three, increased by twenty-two	F. $(a - 22) \div 3$
7. the sum of three and twenty-two, all divided by a number, *a*	G. $(a + 3) \div 22$
8. a number, *a*, less than twenty-two, all times three	H. $(a + 3) \times 22$
9. the sum of a number, *a*, and three, all divided by twenty-two	I. $22 \times a - 3$
10. a number, *a*, decreased by three and then increased by twenty-two	J. $(3 + 22) \div a$

Name _____

Equivalent Algebraic Expressions

Look at each pair of algebraic expressions. The expressions are equivalent. Which property is used to create each equivalent pair? Write *Commutative Property*, *Associative Property*, or *Distributive Property*.

1. $(3a + 2b) + 4c$ or $3a + (2b + 4c)$ __Associative Property__

2. $2(m + n)$ or $2m + 2n$ __Distributive Property__

3. $5x - 5y$ or $5(x - y)$ __Distributive Property__

4. $7w + 5y$ or $5y + 7w$ __Commutative Property__

5. $4q + (r + c)$ or $(4q + r) + c$ __Associative Property__

6. $36h + 36k$ or $36(h + k)$ __Distributive Property__

7. $(wx)y$ or $w(xy)$ __Associative Property__

8. cd or dc __Commutative Property__

9. $3(2r + s)$ or $6r + 3s$ __Distributive Property__

10. $9x + y$ or $y + 9x$ __Commutative Property__

Use the Commutative, Associative, or Distributive Property to write an equivalent form of each algebraic expression. Possible answers are given.

11. $4(a + b)$ __$4a + 4b$__

12. $(x + 3y) + z$ __$x + (3y + z)$__

13. $6q + 2r$ __$2r + 6q$__

14. $5(gh)$ __$(5g)h$__

15. $9(c + d)$ __$9c + 9d$__

16. $7(e + 2f)$ __$7e + 14f$__

17. $3(w - s)$ __$3w - 3s$__

18. $s + 8$ __$8 + s$__

19. $(m + 2n) + p$ __$m + (2n + p)$__

20. yz __zy__

Name _____

Approximating Square Roots

A square with an area of 25 cm² has a side measuring $\sqrt{25}$ cm = 5 cm.

Area =
25 cm²

$\sqrt{25}$ = 5 cm

What is the length of a side of a square with an area of 40 cm²?

Area =
40 cm²

$\sqrt{40}$ = ? cm

The length is $\sqrt{40}$ cm. Since 40 is not a perfect square, $\sqrt{40}$ is not a whole number. To approximate $\sqrt{40}$, find the two perfect squares closest to 40, one greater than 40 and one less than 40.

The perfect squares are 36 and 49.

$\sqrt{36} < \sqrt{40} < \sqrt{49}$

$6 < \sqrt{40} < 7$

So, the length is between 6 cm and 7 cm. Since 40 is closer to 36 than it is to 49, the length is closer to 6 cm than it is to 7 cm.

Give the whole number closest to each square root.

1. $\sqrt{7}$ _____3_____   2. $\sqrt{15}$ _____4_____   3. $\sqrt{60}$ _____8_____

4. $\sqrt{75}$ _____9_____   5. $\sqrt{5}$ _____2_____   6. $\sqrt{86}$ _____9_____

7. $\sqrt{31}$ _____6_____   8. $\sqrt{22}$ _____5_____   9. $\sqrt{125}$ _____11_____

10. $\sqrt{56}$ _____7_____   11. $\sqrt{2}$ _____1_____   12. $\sqrt{71}$ _____8_____

13. $\sqrt{109}$ _____10_____   14. $\sqrt{24}$ _____5_____   15. $\sqrt{91}$ _____10_____

Name _____

Challenging Equations

For each exercise, four equations are given. Choose the two equations that can be used to solve the problem.

1. How many weeks will you need to work in order to earn $340.50 if you earn $56.75 per week? C, D

   A $340.50 - n = 56.75$

   B $340.50 = n + 56.75$

   C $\dfrac{340.50}{n} = 56.75$

   D $56.75n = 340.5$

2. Three and one-half cups of milk were poured from a container. There were 5 cups left in the container. How many cups of milk were originally in the container? A, C

   A $c - 3\dfrac{1}{2} = 5$

   B $5 - c = 3\dfrac{1}{2}$

   C $3\dfrac{1}{2} + 5 = c$

   D $c + 5 = 3\dfrac{1}{2}$

3. A number multiplied by 1.4 is 9.8. Find the number. A, D

   A $1.4w = 9.8$

   B $\dfrac{w}{9.8} = 1.4$

   C $9.8w = 1.4$

   D $\dfrac{9.8}{w} = 1.4$

4. Anthony sold his used pair of in-line skates for $45 less than he paid for them. If he sold the skates for $65.50, how much did Anthony originally pay for them? B, D

   A $65.50 - x = 45$

   B $x - 65.50 = 45$

   C $x + 45 = 65.50$

   D $x - 45 = 65.50$

5. The width of a rectangle is 4 cm less than the length. If the width is 7.2 cm, what is the rectangle's length? C, D

   A $y + 4 = 7.2$

   B $7.2 - y = 4$

   C $y - 4 = 7.2$

   D $y = 4 + 7.2$

6. The length of the base of a triangle is $\dfrac{1}{3}$ the height. If the height is 9 in., what is the base? A, C

   A $3b = 9$

   B $9b = 3$

   C $\dfrac{9}{3} = b$

   D $\dfrac{b}{9} = 3$

7. Elizabeth is saving to buy 4 tickets to a concert. The cost is $76. If she has already saved $47, how much more does she need? B, D

   A $s - 47 = 76$

   B $s + 47 = 76$

   C $4s = 76$

   D $76 - s = 47$

8. Drew Middle School has 873 students. There are 39 fewer students than last year. How many students were in Drew last year? A, D

   A $n = 873 + 39$

   B $n + 39 = 873$

   C $n = 873 - 39$

   D $n - 39 = 873$

Equivalent Equations

Equivalent equations are equations that have the same solution. For each set of equations, decide which, if any, are equivalent. Write the letters of the equivalent equations.

1. **A** $s + 17 = 31$ **B** $s + 12 = 24$ **C** $s + 63 = 77$ <u>A, C</u>

2. **D** $62 + x = 91$ **E** $x + 19 = 48$ **F** $32 + x = 63$ <u>D, E</u>

3. **G** $2\frac{1}{2} = m + \frac{1}{4}$ **H** $4\frac{1}{4} = m + 2$ **J** $12\frac{3}{4} = 10\frac{1}{2} + m$ <u>G, H, J</u>

4. **A** $6 + w = 13$ **B** $8 + w = 24$ **C** $12 + w = 19$ <u>A, C</u>

5. **D** $a + 28 = 33$ **E** $a + 107 = 112$ **F** $201 + a = 206$ <u>D, E, F</u>

6. **G** $n + \frac{1}{2} = 3$ **H** $n + 4\frac{1}{2} = 6$ **J** $n + 8 = 9\frac{1}{2}$ <u>H, J</u>

7. **A** $y + 2.5 = 9$ **B** $y + 4.5 = 7$ **C** $y + 7 = 9.5$ <u>B, C</u>

8. **D** $43 = h + 6$ **E** $104 = h + 67$ **F** $90 = h + 37$ <u>D, E</u>

9. **G** $p + 6 = 33$ **H** $p + 3 = 30$ **J** $p + 9 = 36$ <u>G, H, J</u>

10. **A** $16\frac{1}{3} = t + 4$ **B** $26\frac{2}{3} = t + 14\frac{1}{3}$ **C** $18 = t + 8\frac{1}{3}$ <u>A, B</u>

11. **D** $6.2 + k = 9$ **E** $k + 1.7 = 3.5$ **F** $2.4 + k = 5.2$ <u>D, F</u>

12. Describe how you decided which equations in each set were equivalent.

<u>Possible answer: I solved each equation in each set.</u>

<u>Then I checked to see which equations in the set had</u>

<u>the same solutions.</u>

_____

Balancing Act

Study the first two scales. Then answer the question to find what is needed to balance the third scale.

1.

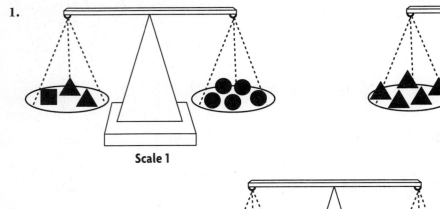

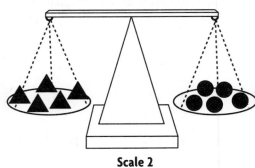

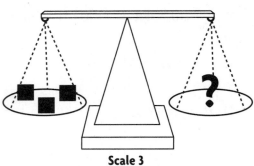

How many circles are needed to balance the 3 squares? _____ 9 circles _____

2.

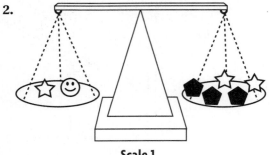

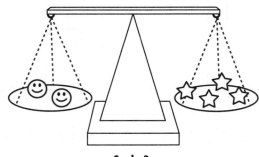

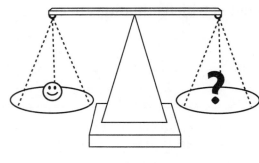

How many pentagons are needed to balance the 1 smiling face? _____ 6 pentagons _____

Riddle Solvers

Here are some riddles that can be solved by writing and solving equations. First write an equation. Then solve it to find the answer to the riddle.

1. When you subtract 50 from this number and then add 15, the result is 95. What is the mystery number?

Equation: _____ $m - 50 + 15 = 95$ _____

Answer: _____ 130 _____

2. Everybody is trying to guess Jerry's age. He says, "If you add 110 to my age, the result is 128." How old is Jerry?

Equation: _____ $a + 110 = 128$ _____

Answer: _____ 18 years old _____

3. Fiona was born in May. She circles her birthday on the calendar and adds 25. The result is 32. When is her birthday?

Equation: _____ $b + 25 = 32$ _____

Answer: _____ May 7 _____

4. Henry is $62\frac{1}{2}$ in. tall. His height is equal to his shoe size plus $49\frac{1}{2}$ in. What is Henry's shoe size?

Equation: $49\frac{1}{2} + s = 62\frac{1}{2}$

Answer: _____ size 13 _____

5. When you subtract this number from 29.3 and then add 12, the result is 22. What is the mystery number?

Equation: _____ $29.3 - g + 12 = 22$ _____

Answer: _____ 19.3 _____

6. Jim, Marilee, and Sonia bought plane tickets. Together they spent $870. Jim's ticket cost $235, and Marilee's ticket cost $50 more than Jim's ticket. How much did Sonia's ticket cost?

Equation: $235 + (235 + 50) + t = 870$

Answer: _____ $350 _____

7. Rico says he is 7 years younger than his brother. If Rico is 26 years old, how old is his brother?

Equation: _____ $r - 7 = 26$ _____

Answer: _____ 33 years old _____

8. Helena subtracted the number of students in her math class from 100 and then added 57. The result is 129. How many students are in Helena's math class?

Equation: _____ $100 - x + 57 = 129$ _____

Answer: _____ 28 students _____

A Spotty Riddle

Solve each equation. Then put the letter of the variable above its value to answer the riddle.

$\frac{b}{2} = 5; b =$ _____ 10 _____ 　　　　$\frac{r}{3} = 3; r =$ _____ 9 _____

$3g = 6; g =$ _____ 2 _____ 　　　　　$2f = 10; f =$ _____ 5 _____

$\frac{i}{4} = 3; i =$ _____ 12 _____ 　　　　$\frac{m}{5} = 3; m =$ _____ 15 _____

$3o = 18; o =$ _____ 6 _____ 　　　　$3y = 9; y =$ _____ 3 _____

$\frac{n}{2} = 8; n =$ _____ 16 _____ 　　　　$\frac{v}{4} = 2; v =$ _____ 8 _____

$4l = 16; l =$ _____ 4 _____ 　　　　$2c = 14; c =$ _____ 7 _____

$\frac{p}{2} = 7; p =$ _____ 14 _____ 　　　　$\frac{a}{3} = 6; a =$ _____ 18 _____

$\frac{t}{5} = 4; t =$ _____ 20 _____ 　　　　$\frac{e}{2} = 11; e =$ _____ 22 _____

How does a leopard change its spots?

$\frac{b}{10}$ $\frac{y}{3}$ 　 $\frac{m}{15}$ $\frac{o}{6}$ $\frac{v}{8}$ $\frac{i}{12}$ $\frac{n}{16}$ $\frac{g}{2}$

$\frac{f}{5}$ $\frac{r}{9}$ $\frac{o}{6}$ $\frac{m}{15}$ 　 $\frac{p}{14}$ $\frac{l}{4}$ $\frac{a}{18}$ $\frac{c}{7}$ $\frac{e}{22}$

$\frac{t}{20}$ $\frac{o}{6}$ 　 $\frac{p}{14}$ $\frac{l}{4}$ $\frac{a}{18}$ $\frac{c}{7}$ $\frac{e}{22}$

CW60 Challenge

Make a Spiral

Pilots use vectors to show both direction and distance.
Draw a vector as an arrow.

Draw the vector (9, 30°).

- Measure 30° counterclockwise from 0°.
- Draw an arrow 9 units long from the center of the circle.
- Label the angle and the vector.

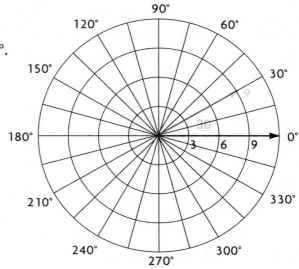

Draw each vector. When you finish, you will have made a spiral.

1. (8, 180°)	**2.** (3, 30°)	**3.** (4, 60°)	**4.** (9, 210°)
5. (5, 90°)	**6.** (12, 300°)	**7.** (11, 270°)	**8.** (6, 120°)
9. (7, 150°)	**10.** (13, 330°)	**11.** (14, 0°)	**12.** (10, 240°)

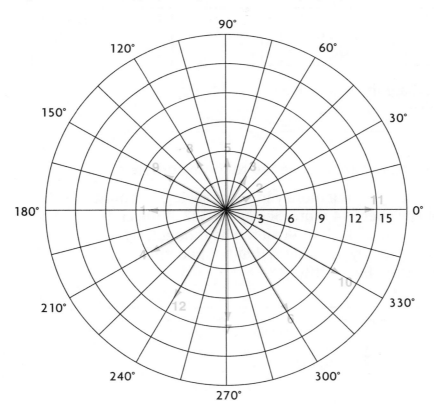

Name _____

Accounting for Money

Ben put one-half of his birthday money into his college account. He spent $18.50 at the music store. At lunch, his sister gave him $3.00. Then Ben spent $8.50 for a movie ticket and snacks. At the end of the day he only had $13.00 left. He thought, "Hey, where did all my money go?" Help Ben account for his money.

1. What do you have to find out?

   how much birthday money Ben had

2. What information do you know?

   $13.00 left at end of day, $8.50 spent at movies and

   $18.50 spent at the music store, additional $3.00 from

   sister, 1/2 the original amount is put away for savings

3. Fill in the working forward and the working backward diagrams.

birthday money, b	÷ 2	=	spending money, s		spending money	−	music store	+	sister	−	movie	=	money left
b	÷ 2	=	s		s	−	$18.50	+	$3.00	−	$8.50	=	$13.00

money left	+	movie	−	sister	+	music store	=	spending money, s		$2 \times s$	=	birthday money, b
$13.00	+	$8.50	−	$3.00	+	$18.50	=	$37.00			=	$74.00

   $2 \times 37

4. Choose one of the diagrams and solve the problem.

   Students may use either diagram. $s = $37; b = 74

Draw a working backward diagram to solve the following problem.

5. Ellie put half of her baby-sitting money into her savings account. At lunch, her aunt gave her $14 more. She spent $22 at the craft store. At the end of the day she had $40 left. She thought, "Hey, I thought I spent more money than this. What happened?" How much did Ellie earn from baby-sitting?

   $96

money left	+	craft store	−	aunt's gift	=	spending money, s		$2 \times s$	=	original amount
$40	+	$22	−	$14	=	$48		$2 \times 48	=	$96

© Harcourt

Name _____

Which Is Heaviest?

List the items on the scales from lightest to heaviest.

1.

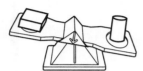

rectangular box, cylinder,

triangular box

2.

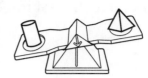

rectangular box, triangular box,

cylinder

3.

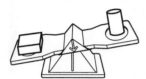

cylinder, rectangular box,

triangular box

4.

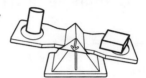

triangular box, cylinder,

rectangular box

5.

cylinder, triangular box,

rectangular box

6.

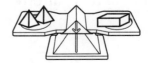

triangular box, rectangular box,

cylinder

Curious Patterns

1. Complete the first three equations. Look for a pattern. Then use the pattern to complete the last three equations.

$(3 \times 11) + (3 \times 1) =$ _____36_____

$(3 \times 10) + (3 \times 2) =$ _____36_____

$(3 \times 9) + (3 \times 3) =$ _____36_____

$(3 \times$ __8__$) + (3 \times$ __4__$) =$ _____36_____

$(3 \times$ __7__$) + (3 \times$ __5__$) =$ _____36_____

$(3 \times$ __6__$) + (3 \times$ __6__$) =$ _____36_____

2. Look for a pattern to complete each equation.

$9 \times 1 + 2 =$ _____11_____

$9 \times 12 + 3 =$ _____111_____

$9 \times 123 + 4 =$ _____1,111_____

$9 \times 1,234 + 5 =$ _____11,111_____

$9 \times 12,345 + 6 =$ _____111,111_____

$9 \times 123,456 + 7 =$ _____1,111,111_____

$9 \times$ ____1,234,567____ $+$ ____8____ $=$ ____11,111,111____

$9 \times$ ____12,345,678____ $+$ ____9____ $=$ ____111,111,111____

$9 \times$ ____123,456,789____ $+$ ____10____ $=$ ____1,111,111,111____

3. Draw the next figure in this pattern.

 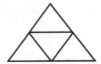 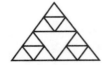 

Name _____

Operation 42

Each circle has four numbers. If you perform three different operations on them, the final result is 42. The first one has been done for you.

1.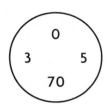

A. _____ $70 \div 5 = 14$ _____

B. _____ $14 \times 3 = 42$ _____

C. _____ $42 - 0 = 42$ _____

2.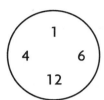

A. _____ $12 \times 4 = 48$ _____

B. _____ $48 - 6 = 42$ _____

C. _____ $42 \div 1 = 42$ _____

3.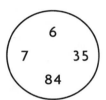

A. _____ $84 \div 6 = 14$ _____

B. _____ $14 + 35 = 49$ _____

C. _____ $49 - 7 = 42$ _____

4.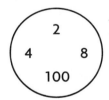

A. _____ $100 \div 4 = 25$ _____

B. _____ $25 \times 2 = 50$ _____

C. _____ $50 - 8 = 42$ _____

5.

A. _____ $30 \div 5 = 6$ _____

B. _____ $6 \times 7 = 42$ _____

C. _____ $42 - 0 = 42$ _____

6.

A. _____ $5 + 8 = 13$ _____

B. _____ $13 \times 4 = 52$ _____

C. _____ $52 - 10 = 42$ _____

7.

A. _____ $17 \times 3 = 51$ _____

B. _____ $51 - 14 = 37$ _____

C. _____ $37 + 5 = 42$ _____

Circle 5: 0, 5, 7, 30
Circle 6: 4, 5, 8, 10
Circle 7: 3, 5, 14, 17

Challenge   CW65

Two Functions Are Better Than One

A function can be written as two different equations, one equation for each variable. Write two equations for the function represented by each of the tables below. Then use one of the equations to answer the question.

pounds *(p)*	1	2	3	4	5
ounces *(o)*	16	32	48	64	80

1. $o =$ _____ $16 \times p$ _____   2. $p =$ _____ $o \div 16$ _____

3. If you have a package that weighs 24 oz, how many pounds does it weigh? _____ $1\frac{1}{2}$ lb _____

number of hours *(h)*	2	4	6	8
number of minutes *(m)*	120	240	360	480

4. $m =$ _____ $60 \times h$ _____   5. $h =$ _____ $m \div 60$ _____

6. If you work for $2\frac{3}{4}$ hr, how many minutes do you work? _____ 165 min _____

length *(l)*	4	8	12	16	20
width *(w)*	1	3	5	7	9

7. $w =$ _____ $l \div 2 - 1$ or $(l - 2) \div 2$ _____   8. $l =$ _____ $2w + 2$ or $(w + 1) \times 2$ _____

9. If the length of a rectangle is 10 in., how wide is it? _____ 4 in. _____

miles *(m)*	20	30	40	50	60
hours *(h)*	13	18	23	28	33

10. $h =$ _____ $m \div 2 + 3$ or $(m + 6) \div 2$ _____   11. $m =$ _____ $2h - 6$ or $(h - 3) \times 2$ _____

12. If you spend 30 hr traveling, how many miles will you go? _____ 54 mi _____

What's the Score?

A scoreboard may use rectangular patterns
of lights to form numbers and letters.

At the right are grids with squares shaded to form
a 7 and an *A*.

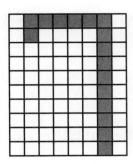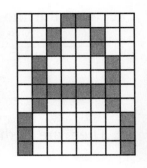

1. On the grids below, give the score of a basketball game.
   Form the numbers by shading squares on the grids.
   Answers will vary.

Team 1   Team 2

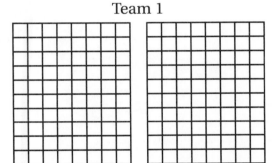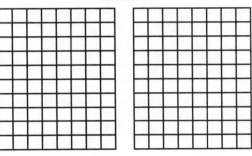

2. On the grid below, write your first or last name using patterns.
   Experiment! Check students' work.

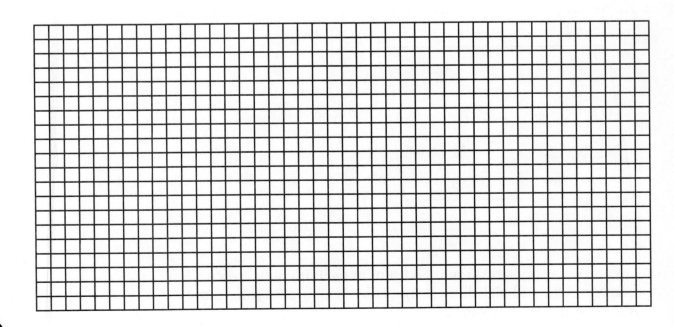

Challenge CW67

Let Me Count the Ways

1. Name the line in 12 different ways.

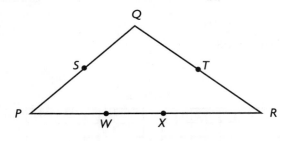

<u>$\overleftrightarrow{AB}$, $\overleftrightarrow{BA}$, $\overleftrightarrow{BC}$, $\overleftrightarrow{CB}$, $\overleftrightarrow{CD}$, $\overleftrightarrow{DC}$, $\overleftrightarrow{AC}$, $\overleftrightarrow{CA}$, $\overleftrightarrow{BD}$, $\overleftrightarrow{DA}$, $\overleftrightarrow{AD}$, $\overleftrightarrow{DB}$</u>

2. There are 12 different line segments in the figure. Name them.

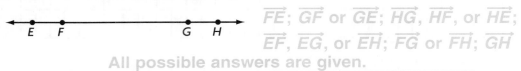

<u>$\overline{PQ}$, $\overline{PS}$, $\overline{SQ}$, $\overline{QT}$, $\overline{TR}$, $\overline{QR}$, $\overline{PW}$, $\overline{WX}$, $\overline{XR}$, $\overline{PX}$, $\overline{WR}$, $\overline{PR}$</u>

3. Name six different rays in the figure.

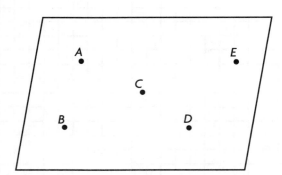

$\overrightarrow{FE}$; $\overrightarrow{GF}$ or $\overrightarrow{GE}$; $\overrightarrow{HG}$, $\overrightarrow{HF}$, or $\overrightarrow{HE}$;
$\overrightarrow{EF}$, $\overrightarrow{EG}$, or $\overrightarrow{EH}$; $\overrightarrow{FG}$ or $\overrightarrow{FH}$; $\overrightarrow{GH}$

All possible answers are given.

4. Name the plane in 10 different ways, using three points each time.

ABC, ABD, ABE, BCD, BCE, ACD, ACE, ADE, BDE, CDE

5. On a ruler, suppose you mark a point at each inch, half inch, quarter inch, and eighth inch. The ruler is 12 inches long. How many points are marked?

96 points

Name _____

Angles Everywhere

Use the figure for Exercises 1–8.

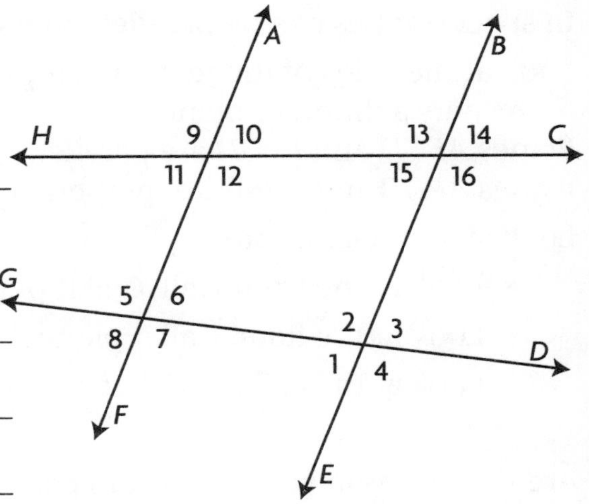

1. Name four lines.

   _AF_, _BE_, _CH_, and _DG_

2. List each pair of vertical angles.

   ∠1 and ∠3; ∠2 and ∠4; ∠5 and ∠7;

   ∠6 and ∠8; ∠9 and ∠12; ∠10 and

   ∠11; ∠13 and ∠16; ∠14 and ∠15

   m∠12 = m∠16 = 120°
   m∠4 = m∠5 = 100°

3. List all the angles that have a measure equal to 120˚.

   ∠9, ∠12, ∠13, ∠16

4. List all the angles that have a measure equal to 100˚.

   ∠2, ∠4, ∠5, ∠7

5. List all the angles that have a measure equal to 60˚.

   ∠10, ∠11, ∠14, ∠15

6. Which angle is larger, ∠6 or ∠10? Explain.

   m∠6 = 80° and m∠10 = 60°, so m∠6 is larger.

7. List two adjacent angles whose measures have a sum greater than 180˚. Explain.

   There are none. The sum of the adjacent angles equals 180°.

8. In the figure above, four lines intersect to form a quadrilateral. What is the sum of the angle measures inside the quadrilateral?

   360˚

9. Draw four intersecting lines to form a different quadrilateral. Measure the angles inside the quadrilateral with a protractor. What is the sum of the angle measures?

   Check students' drawings. 360°

© Harcourt

Challenge CW69

Space Project

In space, planes can be parallel, intersecting, or perpendicular.
Look at the sides of the rectangular prism. Each side
represents a different plane.
Planes *ABCD* and *EFGH* are parallel.
Planes *AEHB* and *AEFD* are perpendicular and intersecting.

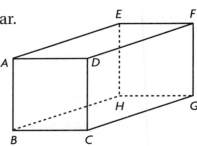

Look at your classroom.

- Look at the front wall. Call it plane 1.
- Look at the floor. Call it plane 2
- Look at the ceiling. Call it plane 3.

Are the planes in your classroom parallel, intersecting, or
perpendicular?

1. planes 1 and 2

____perpendicular____

____and intersecting____

2. planes 2 and 3

____parallel____

_____

3. planes 1 and 3

____perpendicular____

____and intersecting____

For Exercises 4–8, use the figure at the right.
Tell whether the planes are parallel, intersecting, or perpendicular.

4. plane *BCFG* and plane *ABCD*
____perpendicular and intersecting____

5. plane *ABGH* and plane *DCFE*
____parallel____

6. plane *HGFE* and plane *BCFG*
____perpendicular and intersecting____

7. plane *ADEH* and plane *ABGH*
____perpendicular and intersecting____

8. plane *ABCD* and plane *HGFE*
____parallel____

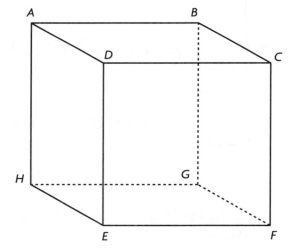

9. Give an example of planes that intersect but are not perpendicular.

____Possible answer: the lateral faces of a triangular prism____

Name _____

Polygon Stars

You can create stars inside polygons. Start with a regular polygon.
Draw line segments connecting vertices, as shown below.

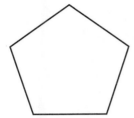 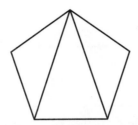 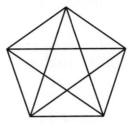

1. Create a star inside the polygon below. What is the name of the
   polygon?

   _____ hexagon

   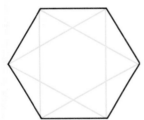

2. Use the polygons below to create 2 different stars. What is the
   name of the polygon?

   _____ octagon

    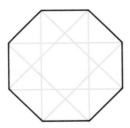

3. Use the polygons below to create 4 different stars. What is the
   name of the polygon?

   _____ decagon

     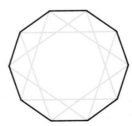 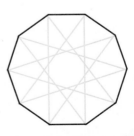

Sometimes, Always, Never

Each statement is either always true, sometimes true, or never true.
Read each statement carefully and write *sometimes, always,* or *never.*

1. A right triangle is a scalene triangle.

   _____ sometimes _____

2. A triangle has two obtuse angles.

   _____ never _____

3. The sum of the measures of the two smallest angles of a triangle
   is less than the measure of the third angle.

   _____ sometimes _____

4. The two acute angles of a right triangle are complementary.

   _____ always _____

5. An acute triangle has three congruent angles.

   _____ sometimes _____

6. Two angles of a triangle are supplementary.

   _____ never _____

7. A scalene triangle has a right angle.

   _____ sometimes _____

8. If two angles of a triangle are acute, the third angle is also an
   acute angle.

   _____ sometimes _____

9. If two angles of a triangle are complementary, the triangle must
   be a right triangle.

   _____ always _____

10. A right triangle has one obtuse angle.

   _____ never _____

Patterns Everywhere

For each number pattern:
- Describe how the pattern might have been created.
- Write the next three possible numbers in the pattern.

In some cases, you may wish to use a calculator to help describe the pattern and to find the next three possible numbers.

1. 16, 14, 12, 10, 8, . . .

   _____Two was subtracted from each number; 6, 4, 2_____

2. 5, 8, 11, 14, 17, . . .

   _____Three was added to each number; 20, 23, 26_____

3. 2, 4, 8, 16, 32, . . .

   _____Each number was doubled or multiplied by 2; 64, 128, 256_____

4. 1,000, 200, 40, 8, 1.6, . . .

   _____Each number was divided by 5; 0.32, 0.064, 0.0128_____

5. 12, 10.5, 9, 7.5, 6, . . .

   _____Each number had 1.5 subtracted from it; 4.5, 3, 1.5_____

6. 4, 5, 9, 14, 23, . . .

   _____Each number is the sum of the previous two numbers; 37, 60, 97_____

7. 5, 6, 8, 11, 15, . . .

   _____Each increase is one more than the previous increase; 20, 26, 33_____

8. 5.25, 7.50, 9.75, 12, . . .

   _____Each number had 2.25 added to it; 14.25, 16.50, 18.75_____

9. 1, 3, 7, 15, 31, . . .

   _____Each number was doubled and 1 was added; 63, 127, 255_____

10. 1, 4, 9, 16, 25, . . .

    _____Square each counting number in order; 36, 49, 64_____

Coordinate Quadrilaterals

On each grid, three points are shown. Name the coordinates of a fourth point that can be used to complete the given figure. Then draw the figure. For some of the figures, there is more than one answer.

1. rectangle

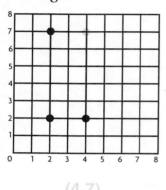

_____ (4,7) _____

2. parallelogram

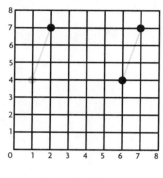

_____ (1,4) _____

3. trapezoid

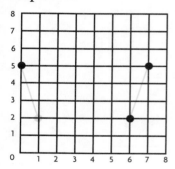

_____ Possible answer: (1,2) _____

4. square

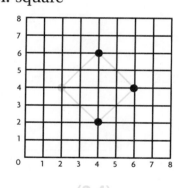

_____ (2,4) _____

5. rhombus

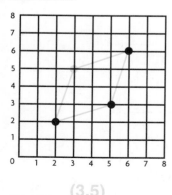

_____ (3,5) _____

6. parallelogram

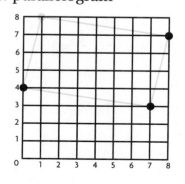

_____ (1,8) _____

© Harcourt

Hidden Figures

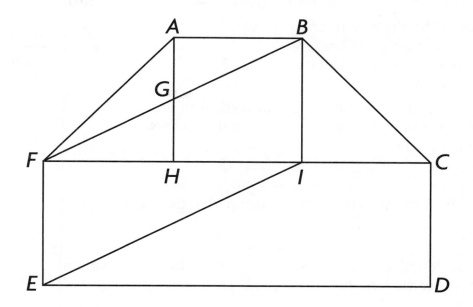

Use the figure to name the following polygons. One or more of the polygons can be used more than once. A ruler may be helpful.

1. A parallelogram with no right angles _____ *BIEF*

2. A parallelogram with four right angles _____ *ABIH or CDEF*

3. A right scalene triangle _____ *BIF, FEI, FGH, or ABG*

4. A right isosceles triangle _____ *AFH or BCI*

5. A rectangle with two pairs of congruent sides _____ *CDEF or ABIH*

6. An obtuse scalene triangle _____ *ABF or BCF*

7. A rectangle with all sides congruent _____ *ABIH*

8. A trapezoid with two congruent sides _____ *ABIF, ABCH, ABCF, BIHG, or ICDE*

9. A pentagon with three congruent sides _____ *ABIEF*

10. A hexagon with three congruent sides and two congruent sides _____ *ABCDEF*

Inscribed Polygons

Use the figure at the right to answer the questions.

The diameter of the circle is 16 cm.
Hexagon *ABCDEF* is a regular hexagon.
All its sides are congruent and all its
angles are congruent.

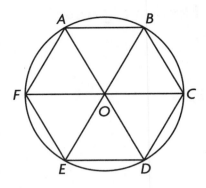

1. A polygon is inscribed in a circle if all vertices of the polygon touch the circle. What types of polygons are inscribed in circle O?

   _____ hexagon, trapezoid _____

2. Explain why there are no triangles inscribed in the circle.

   Possible answer: There are no triangles with all vertices
   _____ touching the circle. _____

3. What is the length of the longer base of trapezoid *ABCF*? Explain how you know the length.

   __ 16 cm; the longer base of trapezoid *ABCF* is a diameter __

   _____ of the circle. _____

4. What is the relationship between the lengths of sides *AO* and *OF* in triangle *AOF*? Explain.

   __ The two sides are congruent; they are radii of the circle __

   _____ and all radii of the same circle are congruent. _____

5. From the information given, can triangle *DOE* be a scalene triangle? Explain.

   ___ No; at least two sides are congruent. In a scalene ___

   _____ triangle, each side has a different length. _____

6. Triangle *BOC* is an equilateral triangle. What is the perimeter of triangle *BOC*?

   _____ 24 cm _____

7. How could you demonstrate that figure *BODC* is a rhombus?

   Possible answer: Show that it is a quadrilateral with four
   _____ congruent sides. _____

8. Find the perimeter of each of the following figures.

   a. hexagon *ABCDEF*   **b.** trapezoid *CDEF*   **c.** rhombus *AOEF*

   _____ 48 cm _____   _____ 40 cm _____   _____ 32 cm _____

Measure Up

Use a ruler and a protractor to measure the sides and angles of each figure. List all pairs of congruent sides or angles for each figure.

1.

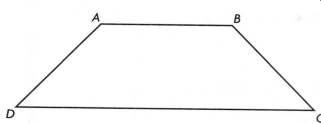

$\overline{AD} \cong \overline{BC}, \angle A \cong \angle B, \angle D \cong \angle C$

2.

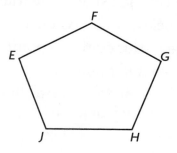

$\overline{EJ} \cong \overline{GH}, \overline{EF} \cong \overline{GF}, \angle J \cong \angle H,$

$\angle E \cong \angle G$

3.

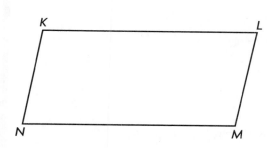

$\overline{KN} \cong \overline{LM}, \overline{KL} \cong \overline{NM}, \angle N \cong \angle L,$

$\angle K \cong \angle M$

4.

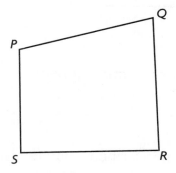

$\overline{SR} \cong \overline{RQ}, \angle S \cong \angle R$

5.

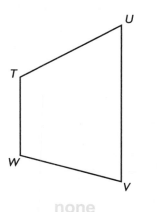

6.

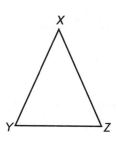

$\overline{XY} \cong \overline{XZ}, \angle Y \cong \angle Z$

Circumscribed Circles and Inscribed Triangles

1. Follow these steps to draw a circumscribed circle around triangle *XYZ*.

   a. Bisect each side of the triangle.

   b. Label the point where the three bisectors intersect as *P*.

   c. Place your compass point on *P*.

   d. Open it to point *X* on the triangle.

   e. Draw a circle with *P* as the center. The circle should touch each vertex of the triangle: *X*, *Y*, and *Z*.   Check students' drawings.

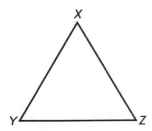

2. Describe the line segments *PX*, *PY*, and *PZ*.

   _____They are the radii of the circle._____

3. Draw an inscribed triangle inside of triangle *ABC* by finding the midpoints of the sides of triangle *ABC* and connecting them.
   Check students' drawings.

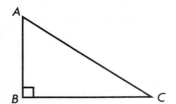

4. Classify the inscribed triangle.

   _____right triangle_____

Odd Figure Out

Select the figure that is not similar to the rest.

1.

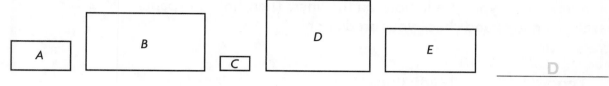

_____ D

2.

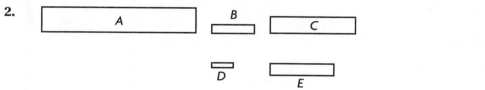

_____ A

3.

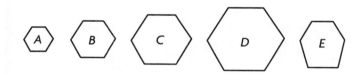

_____ E

4.

_____ C

5.

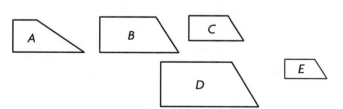

_____ A

6.

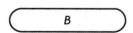

_____ D

Mirror Images

When you look in a mirror, you see a reflection of your image. Look at the letters below. Predict the words they will become if held to a mirror. Write your predictions on the lines. Then, hold the paper against a mirror and check your predictions. Students' predictions may vary.

Letters	Predictions	Words
1. MOM	_____	MOM
2. WOT	_____	TOW
3. XIM	_____	MIX
4. TIH	_____	HIT
5. TAH	_____	HAT
6. XAM	_____	MAX
7. MIT	_____	TIM

Use what you know about reflections to create a secret message to a friend. Write the message below. Be sure to place the letters in such a way that they can be read when reflected in a mirror!
Check students' messages.

Name _____

To Tessellate or Not to Tessellate

One way to determine whether or not a regular polygon will tessellate is to determine if the measure of each angle in the polygon is a factor of 360. If the measure is a factor of 360, then the polygon will tessellate. A square will tessellate because 90 is a factor of 360.

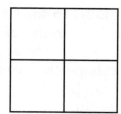

1. Write the factors of 360.

1, 2, 3, 4, 5, 6, 8, 9, 10, 12, 15, 18, 20, 24, 30, 36, 40, 45, 60, 72, 90, 120, 180, 360

Determine if each polygon will tessellate.

2.
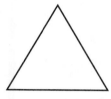

Measure of each interior angle:

60°

Is the angle a factor of 360?

yes

Will this polygon tessellate?

yes

3.

Measure of each interior angle:

108°

Is the angle a factor of 360?

no

Will this polygon tessellate?

no

4.
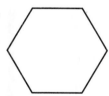

Measure of each interior angle:

120°

Is the angle a factor of 360?

yes

Will this polygon tessellate?

yes

5.

Measure of each interior angle:

135°

Is the angle a factor of 360?

no

Will this polygon tessellate?

no

6. Explain why some regular polygons will not tessellate.

The measure of their interior angles is not a factor of 360.

Name _____

Model the Solution

Draw a model to solve each of the puzzles below. You will need to trace or make copies of each shape.

1. This shape can be cut into two pieces that can be put together to make a trapezoid.

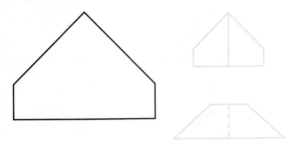

2. This shape can be cut into two pieces that can be put together to make a hexagon.

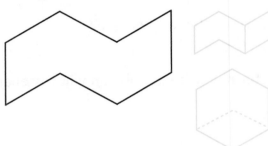

3. Use 4 copies of this shape to make a square.

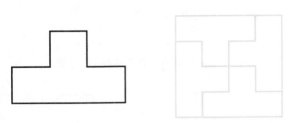

4. Use 2 copies of this shape and 2 copies of the shape from Exercise 3 to make a rectangle.

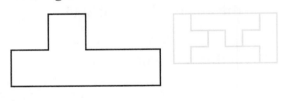

5. Make a square using 2 copies of this shape.

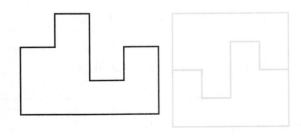

6. This shape can be cut into two pieces that can be put together to make a pentagon.

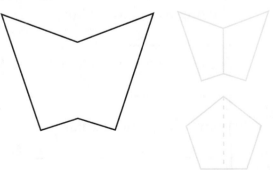

© Harcourt

Symmetry Puzzler

These eight figures are all congruent. They have the same size and shape. Only their positions are different. They contain no line or rotational symmetry, but they can be copied and combined to create symmetric figures.

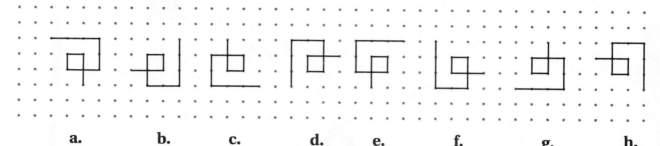

a.　　**b.**　　**c.**　　**d.**　　**e.**　　**f.**　　**g.**　　**h.**

Identify which of the figures have been combined, without overlapping, to create each design. Order of letters may vary.

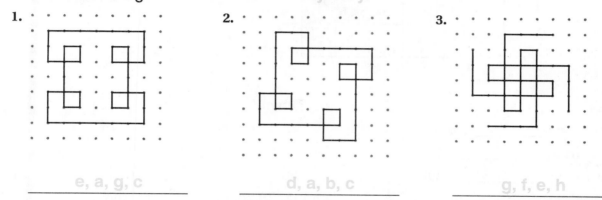

1.　　　　　　　2.　　　　　　　3.

　　e, a, g, c　　　　　　d, a, b, c　　　　　g, f, e, h

Use the figures to create two different symmetric designs of your own. Be sure each one is made from congruent parts in different positions. They may have line symmetry, rotational symmetry, or both.

Check students' drawings.

Measurement Puzzle

Across

1. 31 lb = _____?_____ oz
2. 468 in. = _____?_____ yd
3. 161 days = _____?_____ wk
4. 13 yd = _____?_____ in.
5. 51 qt = _____?_____ c
6. 21 wk = _____?_____ days
7. 12 qt = _____?_____ fl oz
8. 129 gal = _____?_____ qt
9. 45 wk = _____?_____ days
10. 53 qt = _____?_____ c
11. 11 hr = _____?_____ min
12. 12 qt = _____?_____ pt
13. 117 yd = _____?_____ ft
14. 6 T = _____?_____ lb
15. 5 mi = _____?_____ ft

Down

1. 18 days = _____?_____ hr
4. 9 mi = _____?_____ ft
11. 80 c = _____?_____ fl oz
12. 29 wk = _____?_____ days
13. 62 c = _____?_____ pt
14. $9\frac{1}{2}$ ft = _____?_____ in.
16. 79 gal = _____?_____ qt
17. 7 gal = _____?_____ fl oz
18. 34 gal = _____?_____ fl oz
19. 12 gal = _____?_____ c
20. 50 pt = _____?_____ qt
21. 12 lb = _____?_____ oz

Name _____

Math Tip Puzzle

Match each metric measurement in Column 1 with an equivalent measure in Column 2. Then write each corresponding letter on the lines below marked with the exercise number to discover the Math Tip.

Column 1

L _____	**1.** 17 kg
R _____	**2.** 25 mL
E _____	**3.** 500 dm
T _____	**4.** 200 cg
A _____	**5.** 615 cm
N _____	**6.** 170 dg
O _____	**7.** 0.25 L
U _____	**8.** 0.5 km
V _____	**9.** 2,000 g
M _____	**10.** 0.615 km
D _____	**11.** 1.7 g
H _____	**12.** 250 L
I _____	**13.** 5,000 m
P _____	**14.** 0.2 kg
S _____	**15.** 61,500 mm
C _____	**16.** 20 g

Column 2

(A)	6.15 m
(C)	200 dg
(D)	170 cg
(E)	50 m
(H)	2,500 dL
(I)	5 km
(L)	17,000 g
(M)	615 m
(N)	17 g
(O)	250 mL
(P)	2,000 dg
(R)	0.025 L
(S)	61.5 m
(T)	2 g
(U)	5,000 dm
(V)	2 kg

M O V E   T H E
10 7 9 3   4 12 3

D E C I M A L   P O I N T
11 3 16 13 10 5 1   14 7 13 6 4

T O   C O N V E R T
4 7   16 7 6 9 3 2 4

M E T R I C   U N I T S .
10 3 4 2 13 16   8 6 13 4 15

Challenge   CW85

Name _____

A European Vacation

Solve. Possible explanations are given.

1. When Carol claims her luggage at the airport in Europe, she discovers that the latch is broken. She needs to buy tape to hold the suitcase closed. She estimates that she needs about 12 ft of tape. Which length of tape should she buy: 2 m, 4 m, or 6 m? Explain your reasoning.

   4 m; since 1 ft ≈ 30 cm, 12 ft ≈ 360 cm, and 360 cm = 3.6 m

2. While driving on a highway, Carol sees a sign that reads "Paris 200 km." She reads the customary scale on the speedometer and sees that she is driving at 60 mi per hr. At that rate, will she reach Paris in 3 hr? If not, about how long will she need? Explain how you decided.

   Yes, she will be able to reach Paris in less than 3 hr. Since

   1 mi ≈ 1.6 km, divide 200 by 1.6 to find that 200 km ≈ 125 mi.

   At 60 mi per hr, she will be able to reach Paris in about 2 hr.

3. Carol is renting an apartment in Paris. She plans to invite five friends to dinner. She needs $\frac{1}{2}$ lb of meat per person to make hamburgers. At the supermarket, she buys a package of meat that weighs 1 kg. Has she bought enough for six people, or does she need to buy more? Explain your reasoning.

   She will need to buy more meat. She needs 3 lb of meat and

   1 kg ≈ 2.2 lb. She needs to buy about 0.35 kg more meat.

4. Along with the hamburgers, Carol wants to make spaghetti. When she cooks 1 lb of pasta at home, she uses a pot that holds 5 qt of water. She looks over the supply of pots in her rented apartment. There are pots with the following capacities written on their handles: 2 L, 3 L, and 5 L. Which pot is closest to the size Carol uses at home? How do you know?

   The 5 L pot is closest to the 5 qt pot she uses because 1 L

   and 1 qt are almost equivalent measurements.

© Harcourt

How Precise?

Whenever you measure, the smaller the unit you use, the more precise your measurement will be. For any unit that you choose, the *precision* of your measurement is one unit. If you measure correctly, the *greatest possible error* that you can make is one-half of that unit.

You measure the length of a piece of wood and find it to be 18 in. The following are all true:

- The unit you have chosen is an inch.
- The precision of your measurement is 1 in.
- The greatest possible error in your measurement is $\frac{1}{2}$ in. or 0.5 in. So, the length of the piece of wood could be any measurement between 17.5 in. and 18.5 in.

You weigh an apple and find that its weight is 7.6 oz. The following are all true:

- The unit is a tenth of an ounce or 0.1 oz.
- The precision is 0.1 oz.
- The greatest possible error is $\frac{1}{2}$ of 0.1, or 0.05 oz. So, the weight of the apple is between 7.55 oz and 7.65 oz.

For each measurement described below, name the unit that is being used, the precision of the measurement, and the greatest possible error.

1. An apple weighs 6 oz.

    _____ounce; 1 oz; 0.5 oz_____

2. The height of a chair is 31 in.

    _____inch; 1 in.; 0.5 in._____

3. A bottle holds 180 mL of milk.

    _____milliliter; 1 mL; 0.5 mL_____

4. A textbook weighs 2.4 lb.

    _____tenth of a pound; 0.1 lb; 0.05 lb_____

5. A boy is 5 ft tall.

    _____foot; 1 ft; 0.5 ft_____

6. Two towns are 5.8 mi apart.

    _____tenth of a mile; 0.1 mi; 0.05 mi_____

7. An insect is 18 mm long.

    _____millimeter; 1 mm; 0.5 mm_____

8. A barrel weighs 102.5 lb.

    _____half a pound; 0.5 lb; 0.25 lb_____

9. A rug is $16\frac{1}{2}$ ft long.

    _____half a foot; $\frac{1}{2}$ ft; $\frac{1}{4}$ ft_____

10. Two cities are 129.4 km apart.

    _____tenth of a kilometer;_____

    _____0.1 km; 0.05 km_____

Over, Under, or Exact?

For each problem, decide whether an exact answer or an estimate is appropriate. If an exact answer is required, solve the problem. If an estimate is appropriate, decide whether an overestimate or underestimate makes more sense. Then solve the problem. Finally, explain how you made your decisions. Possible explanations are given.

1. A class of 25 students is about to get on a museum elevator when the teacher notices a sign that reads "Maximum Weight 2,500 Pounds." The teacher estimates that the students' average weight is 100 lb. Is it safe for the entire class and teacher to get on the elevator together?

   Overestimate; no. Estimate because it is only necessary to

   compare the students' combined weight to 2,500 lb. The teacher

   should overestimate the students' weight to be on the safe side.

2. For a school trip, 28 students contributed $3.25 each for bus fare and $1.50 each for admission to a museum. At the museum, the students' average lunch cost was $2.50. The principal asked the teacher how much the trip cost so that she could report this information to the Parents' Association. What was the teacher's answer?

   Exact; $203. The principal needed an exact answer because

   she had to report that number to other people.

3. As she is shopping at a supermarket, Kerry is trying to keep track of how much she is spending. She has 3 boxes of cereal that each costs $3.49, 2 rolls of paper towels that each costs $1.89, and 5 cans of vegetables that each costs $0.79. She is wondering whether she has already spent more than the $20 she has with her. Will these purchases total more than $20?

   Overestimate; no. She should overestimate the prices to be

   sure that she will have enough money to pay for her purchases

   when she reaches the checkout.

4. John has been saving money for a new pair of $55 sneakers. He has $23 in a sock, $12 in one drawer, $18 under his bed, and $17 in his backpack. Has John saved enough money to pay for the sneakers?

   Underestimate; yes. John should underestimate the amount

   he has saved to make sure he will have enough money.

© Harcourt

Designing Figures

Use the information to design a figure with the given perimeter. Be sure
to label the length of each side of your figure. Check students' drawings.

1. A rectangle with a perimeter of 62 ft

2. A pentagon with a perimeter of 30 cm

3. An irregular figure with 7 sides and a perimeter of 78 m

4. A trapezoid with a perimeter of 45.2 mi

5. An octagon with a perimeter of 38.4 cm

6. An irregular figure with 6 sides and a perimeter of 99.3 ft

7. A pentagon with a perimeter of 87.5 m

8. A parallelogram with a perimeter of 84.2 ft

Name _____

In the Garden

The Jordans want to tile a part of their backyard. They have
ordered 64 square tiles that measure 2 ft on each side.
When the tiled section is complete, they plan to line it with
potted plants. They will leave one 4 ft opening as an entrance.

☐ 2 ft   2 ft
☐

2 ft ☐

Solve. You may wish to experiment with square tiles.

1. Describe how the Jordans should arrange the tiles in order to use the
   least number of plants to line the tiled area.

   They should arrange the tiles in an 8 tile by 8 tile square.

2. If the Jordans arrange the tiles as you just described, how many feet
   of the tiled section will they need to line with plants?

   They will need to line 60 ft with plants: (2 × 32) − 4

3. Describe how the Jordans should arrange the tiles if they want to
   use the greatest number of plants.

   They should arrange them in a rectangle that is 1 tile wide

   and 64 tiles long.

4. If they arrange the tiles as you just described, how many feet of the
   tiled section will the Jordans need to line with plants?

   They will need to line 256 ft: (2 × 130) − 4

5. If the plants that the Jordans want to use cost $7.50 per foot, what is
   the least they should expect to spend on plants? the most?
   The least they should expect to spend is $450. The most is
   $1,920.

6. If you were going to design a backyard seating area using the 64 tiles,
   describe how you could arrange them differently than the Jordans.

   Possible rectangles: 4 tiles by 16 tiles and 2 tiles by 32 tiles.

7. Find the length of the yard you would need to line with plants to
   surround your designed seating area. Find the cost.

   For 4 tiles × 16 tiles, the length is (2 × 40) − 4 or 76 ft. Cost,

   $570. For 2 tiles × 32 tiles, the length is (2 × 68) − 4 or 132 ft.

   Cost, $990.

© Harcourt

Significant Digits

A **significant digit** is any digit or zero that serves a purpose other than to locate the decimal point in a number. The accuracy of a measurement can be shown by the number of significant digits in the measurement. The greater the number of significant digits, the more accurate the measurement.

Suppose you measure the diameter of a circle with a ruler that shows both centimeters and millimeters. The measurement is 12.3 cm. A friend measures the diameter of the same circle with a ruler that shows only centimeters. The measurement is 12 cm. Which measurement is more accurate? Count the number of digits to find the number of significant digits.

Measurement	12 cm	12.3 cm
Unit of measure	1 cm	0.1 cm
Significant digits	1 and 2	1, 2, and 3
Number of significant digits	2	3

The measurement 12.3 cm has more significant digits than the measurement 12 cm because the diameter was measured using a smaller unit. Therefore, 12.3 cm is the more accurate measurement.

When calculating the circumference of a circle, you can use significant digits to help determine how to round an answer. Round to the same number of significant digits as there were in the measurement of the radius or the diameter.

Find the circumference of the circle with the given diameter. Use $\pi = 3.14$.

Diameter	Number of Significant Digits	Circumference
1. 2 cm	1	6 cm
2. 5.6 in.	2	18 in.
3. 3.23 ft	3	10.1 ft
4. 2.27 m	3	7.13 m
5. 3 ft	1	9 ft
6. 2.154 cm	4	6.764 cm
7. 3.1645 km	5	9.9365 km
8. 12.75 mi	4	40.04 mi

Area and Perimeter Puzzles

The area of each of the rectangles below is 20 cm². Determine the
width of each rectangle. Then find the perimeter of each rectangle.

1.

5 cm

Width: _____4 cm_____

Perimeter: _____18 cm_____

2.

8 cm

Width: _____2.5 cm_____

Perimeter: _____21 cm_____

3.

6.25 cm

Width: _____3.2 cm_____

Perimeter: _____18.9 cm_____

4. If two figures have the same area, do they have to have the same perimeter? Explain.

_____No; there are an unlimited number of perimeters for_____

_____figures that have the same area._____

The perimeter of each of the rectangles below is 50 ft. Determine the
width of each rectangle. Then find the area of each rectangle.

5.

15 ft

Width: _____10 ft_____

Area: _____150 ft²_____

6.

20 ft

Width: _____5 ft_____

Area: _____100 ft²_____

7.

$16\frac{1}{2}$ ft

Width: _____$8\frac{1}{2}$ ft_____

Area: _____$140\frac{1}{4}$ ft²_____

8. If two figures have the same perimeter, do they have to have the same area? Explain.

_____No; there are an unlimited number of areas for figures_____

_____that have the same perimeter._____

The perimeters of several rectangles are given below. Determine the
length and width in whole numbers that will give the greatest area for
each rectangle. Then draw a sketch of the rectangle.

9. Perimeter = 18 in.

Length: _____5 in._____

Width: _____4 in._____

Area: _____20 in.²_____

10. Perimeter = 22 ft

Length: _____6 ft_____

Width: _____5 ft_____

Area: _____30 ft²_____

11. Perimeter = 54 cm

Length: _____14 cm_____

Width: _____13 cm_____

Area: _____182 cm²_____

Drawings will vary, but all figures should be nearly square.

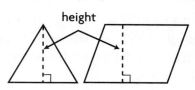
How High

The height of a triangle or parallelogram is needed to find the area of the figure. You can construct the height of a triangle or a parallelogram using a compass and a straightedge.

To construct the height of a triangle, place the compass point on point *A*. Open the compass the length of $\overline{AB}$. Draw an arc through point *B* and $\overline{AC}$.

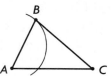

Repeat by placing the compass point on point *C*. Open the compass the length of $\overline{BC}$. Draw an arc through *B* and $\overline{AC}$.

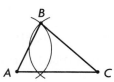

Use a straightedge to draw a line connecting *B* and the intersection of the arcs. Label point *P* where the line intersects $\overline{AC}$. $\overline{BP}$ is the height of the triangle. $\overline{BP} \perp \overline{AC}$.

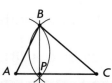

___

To construct the height of a parallelogram, place the compass point on point *A*. Open the compass to more than one-half the length of $\overline{AB}$. Draw an arc across $\overline{AB}$ and $\overline{CD}$.

Keep the same compass opening. Place the compass point on point *B*. Draw another arc through $\overline{AB}$ and $\overline{CD}$.

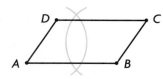

Use a straightedge to draw a line through the points where the arcs intersect. Label point *E* where the line intersects $\overline{CD}$. Label point *F* where the line intersects $\overline{AB}$.

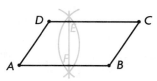

$\overline{EF}$ is the height of the parallelogram and is perpendicular to $\overline{AB}$ and $\overline{CD}$.

Use a compass and straightedge to construct the height of each figure. Then measure the height and find the area of each figure. Check students' work.

1.

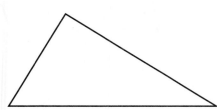

2.

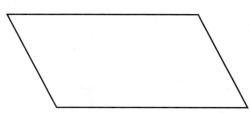

$h = \underline{\text{ 1 in. }}$ $A = \underline{\text{ 1.125 in.}^2}$ $h = \underline{\text{ 1 in. }}$ $A = \underline{\text{ 2 in.}^2}$

Name _____

Attributes and Areas

Length and width are attributes of rectangles. Height is an attribute of triangles and parallelograms. Diameter is an attribute of circles.

Attributes and formulas can be used to estimate the area of a plane figure. Use the attribute of diameter to find the area of a circle. $A = \pi r^2$

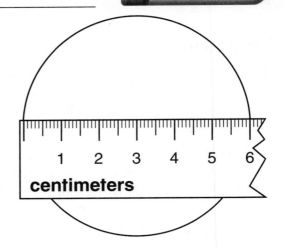

centimeters

First measure the diameter of the circle.

Calculate the radius of the circle.

Then use the formula for the area of a circle.

The area of the circle is 28.26 cm².

$d = 6$ cm
$r = d \div 2$
$r = 3$ cm
$A = \pi r^2$
$A \approx 3.14 \times 3 \times 3$
$A \approx 28.26$ cm²

For each figure, measure the attributes to the nearest tenth of a centimeter. Then calculate the area to the nearest tenth. Use $\pi = 3.14$.

1.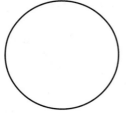

$d = 3$ cm
$A \approx 7.1$ cm²

2.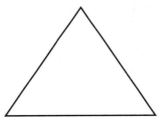

$b = 4$ cm; $h = 3$ cm
$A = 6$ cm²

3.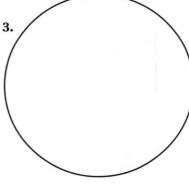

$d = 5$ cm
$A \approx 19.6$ cm²

4.

$l = 6$ cm; $w = 3$ cm
$A = 18$ cm²

5.

$d = 1.5$ cm
$A \approx 1.8$ cm²

6.

$b = 4$ cm; $h = 2$ cm
$A = 8$ cm²

CW94 **Challenge**

Name _____

Formulas and Dimensions

Double the length and width of each original rectangle. Write the new lengths and widths in the appropriate columns under *Doubled Rectangles*. Then find the perimeter and the area of each rectangle, and record your calculations.

ORIGINAL RECTANGLES				DOUBLED RECTANGLES			
Length	Width	Perimeter	Area	Length	Width	Perimeter	Area
1. 3 in.	2 in.	10 in.	6 in.^{2}	6 in.	4 in.	20 in.	24 in.^{2}
2. 5 cm	4 cm	18 cm	20 cm^2	10 cm	8 cm	36 cm	80 cm^2
3. 7 m	1 m	16 m	7 m^2	14 m	2 m	32 m	28 m^2
4. 6 ft	5 ft	22 ft	30 ft^2	12 ft	10 ft	44 ft	120 ft^2

5. Write a formula to show the relationship between the new and the original perimeters of a rectangle when the length and width are doubled.

Possible answer: new perimeter = 2 × original perimeter

6. Write a formula to show the relationship between the new and the original areas of a rectangle when the length and width are doubled.

Possible answer: new area = 4 × original area

Triple the length and width of each original rectangle. Write the new lengths and widths in the appropriate columns under *Tripled Rectangles*. Then find the perimeter and the area of each rectangle, and record your calculations.

ORIGINAL RECTANGLES				TRIPLED RECTANGLES			
Length	Width	Perimeter	Area	Length	Width	Perimeter	Area
7. 3 in.	2 in.	10 in.	6 in.^{2}	9 in.	6 in.	30 in.	54 in.^{2}
8. 5 cm	4 cm	18 cm	20 cm^2	15 cm	12 cm	54 cm	180 cm^2
9. 7 m	1 m	16 m	7 m^2	21 m	3 m	48 m	63 m^2
10. 6 ft	5 ft	22 ft	30 ft^2	18 ft	15 ft	66 ft	270 ft^2

11. Write a formula to show the relationship between the new and the original perimeters of a rectangle when the length and width are tripled.

Possible answer: new perimeter = 3 × original perimeter

12. Write a formula to show the relationship between the new and the original areas of a rectangle when the length and width are tripled.

Possible answer: new area = 9 × original area

© Harcourt

Cross-Figure Puzzle

Use the names of the figures below to complete the puzzle.

Across

1.

2.

3.

4.

5.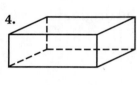

Down

6.

1.

7.

8.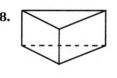

Crossword puzzle:

Across:
1. PENTAGON
2. SQUARE
3. TRIANGLE
4. RECTANGULAR PRISM
5. PYRAMID
6. CONE

Down:
7. CYLINDER
1. PENTAGONAL PYRAMID
8. TRIANGULAR PRISM

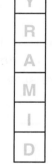
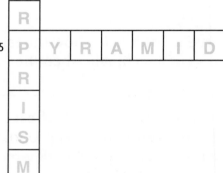
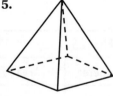

How are the figures shown for 6 Across and 7 Down similar? How are they different?

Both have a circular base and a curved lateral surface;

a cone has 1 base and a vertex; a cylinder has 2 bases and no vertices.

Name _____

What's Your View?

If you fold the net below into a cube, which cubes below are different views of the cube? Write *yes* or *no*.

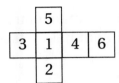

1.

_____ yes _____

2.

_____ yes _____

3.

_____ yes _____

4.

_____ no _____

5.

_____ no _____

6.

_____ yes _____

7.

_____ yes _____

8.

_____ no _____

9.

_____ no _____

10.

_____ yes _____

11.

_____ no _____

12.

_____ yes _____

Name _____

Ornament Creations

A group of students combined solid figures to create unusual ornaments. Read about each student's ornament. Then answer the questions that follow. Possible drawings are shown.

1. For her ornament, Ricki glued together 2 congruent rectangular prisms. Her ornament has 6 faces and 8 vertices.

   • How many edges does her ornament have?

   _____ 12 edges _____

   • Sketch Ricki's ornament.

   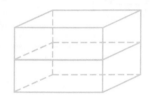
   Prisms could also be glued end-to-end.

2. Seth glued together 2 rectangular pyramids. His ornament has 10 faces and 16 edges.

   • How many vertices does Seth's ornament have?

   _____ 9 vertices _____

   • Sketch Seth's ornament.

   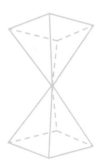

3. Tonya combined a triangular prism and a triangular pyramid that have congruent bases. Her ornament has 7 faces and 12 edges.

   • How many vertices does Tonya's ornament have?

   _____ 7 vertices _____

   • Sketch Tonya's ornament.

   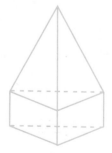

4. Rusty combined a pentagonal prism and a pentagonal pyramid that have congruent bases. His ornament has 11 faces and 11 vertices.

   • How many edges does his ornament have?

   _____ 20 edges _____

   • Sketch Rusty's ornament.

   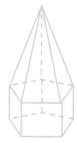

Name _____

Cover That Building!

The Davidsons want to paint the outside of their barn. The numbers of doors and windows are the same on opposite sides of the barn. The Davidsons plan on painting the doors green, the four walls blue, the peaks in front and back yellow, and the roof red. The paint costs $15.87 a gallon. A gallon of paint will cover 345 square feet. How many gallons of each color do they need to buy? How much will it cost them to paint the barn?

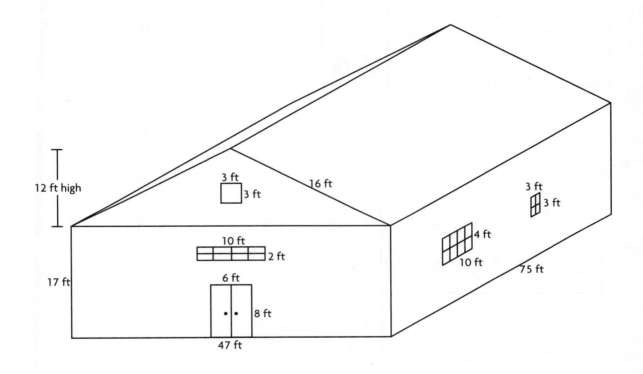

12 ft high

3 ft
3 ft

16 ft

3 ft
3 ft

10 ft
2 ft

4 ft
10 ft

17 ft

6 ft

8 ft

75 ft

47 ft

1 gallon of green paint, 7 gallons of red paint,

2 gallons of yellow paint, 12 gallons of blue paint;

total cost: $349.14

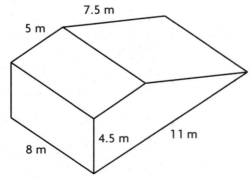

Compound Volumes

Find the volume of each figure.

1.

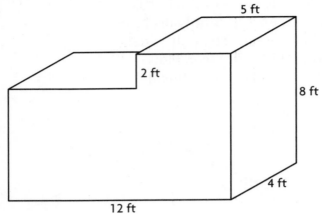

5 ft

2 ft

8 ft

4 ft

12 ft

_____ 328 ft³

2.

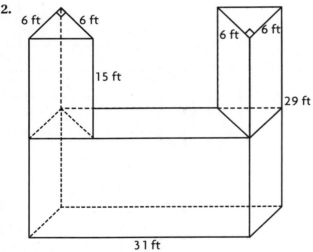

6 ft   6 ft

6 ft   6 ft

15 ft

29 ft

31 ft

_____ 3,144 ft³

3.

7.5 m

5 m

4.5 m   11 m

8 m

_____ 288 m³

After Doubling?

When you double all the dimensions of a rectangular prism, the volume is increased by a factor of 8.

What happens when you triple or quadruple the dimensions of a rectangular prism?

Complete each table.

1.

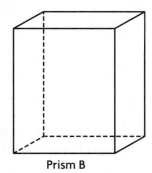

Prism A   Prism B

	Length	Width	Height	Volume
Prism A	3 cm	2 cm	4 cm	24 cm³
Prism B	9 cm	6 cm	12 cm	648 cm³
Ratio: $\frac{B}{A}$	$\frac{9}{3}$, or 3	$\frac{6}{2}$, or 3	$\frac{12}{4}$, or 3	$\frac{648}{24}$, or 27

2.

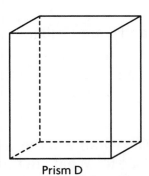

Prism C   Prism D

	Length	Width	Height	Volume
Prism C	3 cm	2 cm	4 cm	24 cm³
Prism D	12 cm	8 cm	16 cm	1,536 cm³
Ratio: $\frac{D}{C}$	$\frac{12}{3}$, or 4	$\frac{8}{2}$, or 4	$\frac{16}{4}$, or 4	$\frac{1,536}{24}$, or 64

Name _____

Pyramid Parts

Find the volume.

1.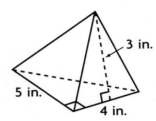

3 in.

5 in.

4 in.

_____ 10 in.³ _____

2.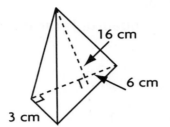

16 cm

6 cm

3 cm

_____ 48 cm³ _____

3.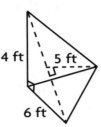

4 ft   5 ft

6 ft

_____ 20 ft³ _____

Solve.

4. Find the volume of the lower portion of the larger pyramid.

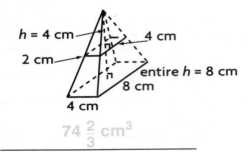

h = 4 cm   4 cm

2 cm

entire h = 8 cm

8 cm

4 cm

74 2/3 cm³

_____

5. Find the volume of the part of the cube that is not part of the pyramid.

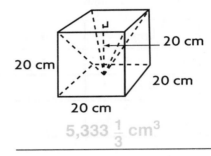

20 cm

20 cm

20 cm

20 cm

5,333 1/3 cm³

_____

6. Explain how the steps for solving Exercises 4 and 5 are similar.

Find the volume of larger figure, then the volume of smaller figure; subtract.

Solve.

7. Find the volume.

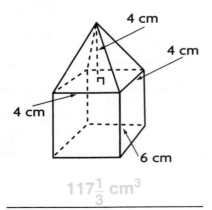

4 cm

4 cm

4 cm

6 cm

117 1/3 cm³

_____

8. The volume of the square pyramid is 282 1/3 ft.³ What are the length and width of the base?

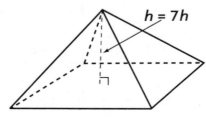

h = 7h

l = 11 ft, w = 11 ft

_____

CW102   Challenge

Name _____

What's Left?

Each cylinder has a hole or holes cut through it. Find the volume that is left. Use 3.14 for π. Round to the nearest whole number.

1.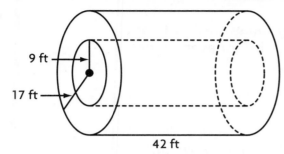

9 ft
17 ft
42 ft

about 27,431 ft³

2.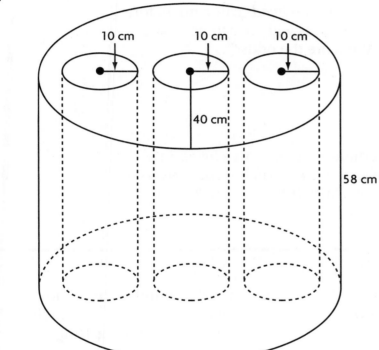

10 cm   10 cm   10 cm
40 cm
58 cm

about 236,756 cm³

3.

6 cm
3 cm
7 cm

about 593 cm³

© Harcourt

What Are The Odds?

People often use *odds* to describe how likely it is that something will occur. Odds are ratios. Drawing a diagram can help you picture what is meant by odds.

- The radio reports, "The odds against rain today are 2 to 1." You can draw a diagram like this, showing 1 "rain" for every 2 "no rains."

RAIN	NO RAIN	NO RAIN

There is a chance of rain. But it is *twice as likely* that it *won't* rain. The odds are 2:1 against rain, and 1:2 for rain.

- Jake tossed a coin five times. Each time *heads* came up. Before the next toss, he stated, "The next toss will *have* to be *tails*. It can't be *heads* again, can it? What are the odds?"

Draw a diagram for *each* toss.

HEADS	TAILS

The coin doesn't "remember" that there have been five *heads* in a row. All that matters is that on the sixth toss, it will be either *heads* or *tails*. Tell Jake that the odds are 50:50 ("fifty-fifty"), or 1 to 1, that heads will come up.

Give the odds.

1. The weather report states that there is a "one in four" chance of snow. Find the odds against snow.

   _____ 3 to 1 _____

2. Jane rolls a number cube with numbers 1, 2, 3, 4, 5, and 6. What are the odds against her getting a 6?

   _____ 5 to 1 _____

3. There are eight teams in the play-offs, and all eight are equally good. What are the odds against a team winning?

   _____ 7 to 1 _____

4. Mr. Harris's house faces the ball field. There are three windows on that side, two ordinary ones and one expensive stained-glass window. All three are the same size. If Hal hits a ball and breaks a window, what are the odds that he breaks the expensive window?

   _____ 1:2 in favor; 2:1 against _____

© Harcourt

Name _____

The Value of a Dollar

	Britain	Canada	China	Israel	Japan	Mexico
Foreign Currency in U.S. Dollars	1.53	0.67	0.12	0.21	0.008	0.10
1 U.S. Dollar in Foreign Currency	0.65	1.53	8.28	4.76	120.16	9.97

The chart shows the recent values of various currencies compared with that of the U.S. dollar. For example:

- A Canadian dollar is worth $0.67 in U.S. dollars, while a U.S. dollar is worth 1.53 Canadian dollars.
- A Mexican peso is worth 10 cents in U.S. dollars, while a U.S. dollar is worth 9.97 Mexican pesos.

(Note: The numbers in the chart change every day. See the business section of a newspaper for today's rates.)

Solve.

1. You have $100 in U.S. dollars. How many units of local currency are worth this amount in each country?

Britain _____65_____   Canada _____153_____

China _____828_____   Israel _____476_____

Japan _____12,016_____   Mexico _____997_____

2. You return from Japan with 1,000 yen. What is this worth in U.S. dollars?

_____$8.00_____

3. A dime is worth about how many Mexican pesos?

_____about 1 peso_____

4. A quarter is worth about how many Japanese yen?

_____about 30 yen_____

5. You make a purchase and receive two quarters in change. Would you prefer that the coins be U.S. or Canadian? Why?

_____Answers will vary. U.S. quarters are worth more than_____

_____Canadian quarters._____

Hidden Similarity

Use the fact that similar figures have corresponding sides with the same ratio to find all rectangles that are similar.

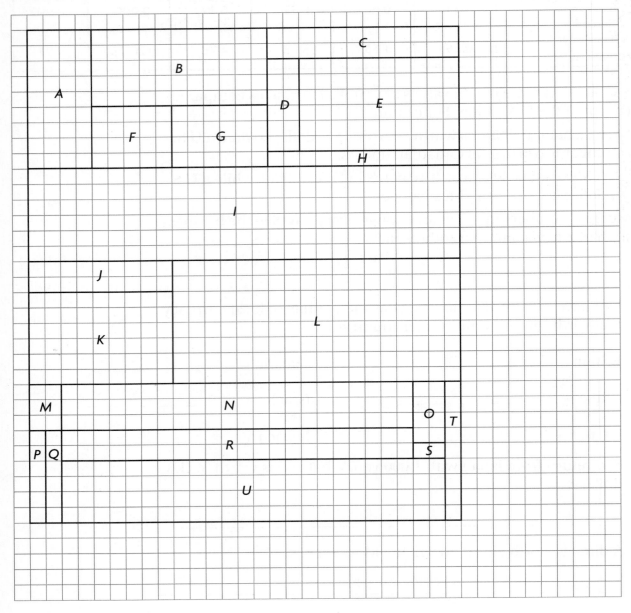

A and L; C, P, U, and Q; O and S; G, K, and M; I and J

Line of Sight

At noon there are hardly any shadows to use for indirect measurement. Instead, you can measure in the following way.

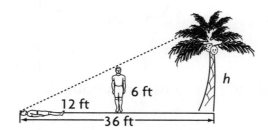

Lie on the ground, and line up the top of an object with the top of another person's head. This creates two similar triangles. You can then form the following proportion:

$$\frac{h}{6} = \frac{36}{12}$$

$$12 \times h = 6 \times 36$$

$$12h = 216$$

$$\frac{12h}{12} = \frac{216}{12}$$

$$h = 18$$

So, $h = 18$ ft.

Find the missing heights in each drawing. Round to the nearest foot.

1.

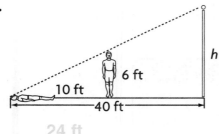

_____24 ft_____

2.

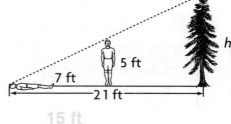

_____15 ft_____

3.

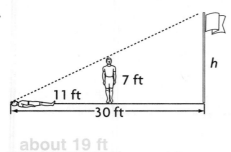

_____about 19 ft_____

4.

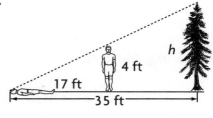

_____about 8 ft_____

Shady Proportions

Some of the proportions in the rectangle below are correct and some are not. Find the errors, and correct them by changing the *last term*.

For example, $\frac{1 \text{ in.}}{3 \text{ ft}} = \frac{6 \text{ in.}}{8 \text{ ft}}$ is wrong. So cross out *8 ft* and write *18 ft*

to form the correct proportion.

Shade in all the squares where you had to correct the proportion. Then describe the shading pattern.

$\frac{1 \text{ in.}}{4 \text{ ft}} = \frac{8 \text{ in.}}{32 \text{ ft}}$	$\frac{1 \text{ cm}}{3 \text{ m}} = \frac{5 \text{ cm}}{25 \text{ m}}$ 15 m	$\frac{1 \text{ cm}}{20 \text{ km}} = \frac{7 \text{ cm}}{140 \text{ km}}$
$\frac{1 \text{ in.}}{8 \text{ ft}} = \frac{4 \text{ in.}}{32 \text{ in.}}$ 32 ft	$\frac{1 \text{ in.}}{9 \text{ ft}} = \frac{10 \text{ in.}}{90 \text{ ft}}$	$\frac{4 \text{ cm}}{1 \text{ mm}} = \frac{2 \text{ cm}}{8 \text{ mm}}$ 0.5 mm
$\frac{1 \text{ in.}}{2 \text{ ft}} = \frac{100 \text{ in.}}{200 \text{ ft}}$	$\frac{1 \text{ cm}}{12 \text{ m}} = \frac{8 \text{ cm}}{48 \text{ m}}$ 96 m	$\frac{1 \text{ in.}}{20 \text{ yd}} = \frac{5 \text{ in.}}{100 \text{ yd}}$
$\frac{1 \text{ cm}}{2.5 \text{ m}} = \frac{4 \text{ cm}}{100 \text{ m}}$ 10 m	$\frac{1 \text{ in.}}{16 \text{ ft}} = \frac{3.5 \text{ in.}}{56 \text{ ft}}$	$\frac{1 \text{ cm}}{3 \text{ m}} = \frac{10 \text{ cm}}{30 \text{ in.}}$ 30 m

Describe the shading pattern.

_____ Alternate squares are shaded, _____

_____ creating a checkerboard pattern. _____

House Plans

The diagram gives the plans for the first floor of a new house. The plans are drawn using the scale 1 in. = 6 ft.

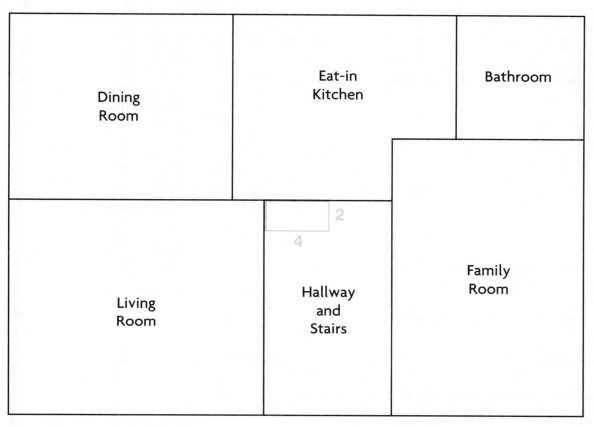

Measure each room. Then find the actual dimensions, to the nearest foot, for the following rooms.

1. Living room _____16 ft × 14 ft_____   **2.** Family room _____18 ft × 12 ft_____

3. Dining room _____14 ft × 12 ft_____   **4.** Bathroom _____8 ft × 8 ft_____

5. A closet is planned in the area marked "Hallway and Stairs." It will be 4 ft wide and 2 ft deep, and will be in the corner bordering the living room and kitchen. Draw the closet to scale on the diagram. See figure above.

6. Label all the dimensions, to the nearest foot, for the eat-in kitchen.

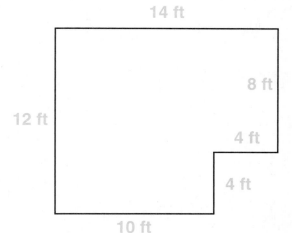

Challenge CW109

In the Shade

Estimate what percent of each figure is shaded.

Then measure by using an inch or centimeter ruler, and calculate the percent that is shaded.

1.

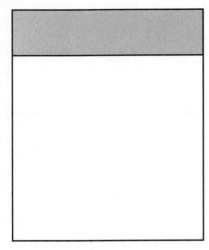

2.

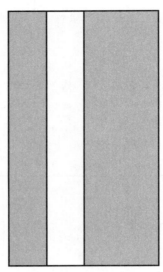

Estimate: ___Answers will vary.___

Actual: ___20%___

Estimate: ___Answers will vary.___

Actual: ___75%___

3. In the space below, draw a rectangle and shade 30% of it. Then draw a circle and shade $66\frac{2}{3}$% of it. Check students' drawings.

Name _____

Strange Dimensions

Find the perimeter of each rectangle. First, however, you need to change the percents to fractions or decimals.

1.

10%

$\frac{3}{10}$

$\frac{8}{10}$ _____

2.

0.25

25%

1 _____

3.

$\frac{1}{8}$

37.5%

1 _____

4.

$\frac{3}{5}$

80%

$2\frac{4}{5}$ _____

5.

0.3

15%

0.9 _____

6.

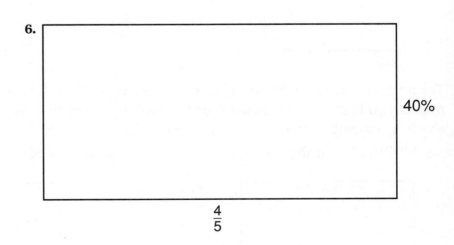

40%

$\frac{4}{5}$

$2\frac{2}{5}$ _____

Challenge CW111

Shady Percents?

You can show 40% of a rectangle by writing it as a fraction.

$40\% = 0.40 = \frac{40}{100} = \frac{4}{10} = \frac{2}{5}$

Then use the fraction to shade the rectangle.

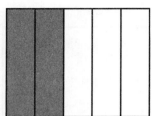

For each exercise, shade the rectangle.

1. 70% of the rectangle

2. 30% of the rectangle

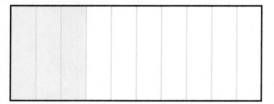

3. 25% of the rectangle

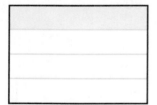

4. 55% of the rectangle

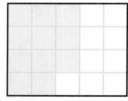

Taking percents of percents is done by working right to left. That means you first find the percent of the rectangle and then you shade a percent of that part of the rectangle.

5. 50% of 25% of the rectangle

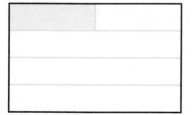

6. 25% of 50% of the rectangle

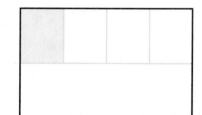

Name _____

Better Buy

Offering discounts helps stores attract customers. Smart customers compare the discounts to see which store is offering the better buy.

Decide which store has the better buy.

1.

STORE "A"
JEANS SALE
REGULARLY $35.78
40% OFF

STORE "B"
JEANS SALE
REGULARLY $57.25
60% OFF

_____ Store A

2.

STORE "A"
SHORTS SALE
REGULARLY $12.75
80% OFF

STORE "B"
SHORTS SALE
REGULARLY $4.25
50% OFF

_____ Store B

3.

STORE "A"
SHOE SALE
REGULARLY $48.90
35% OFF

STORE "B"
SHOE SALE
REGULARLY $52.75
42% OFF

_____ Store B

4.

STORE "A"
BOOT SALE
REGULARLY $88.64
18% OFF

STORE "B"
BOOT SALE
REGULARLY $68.59
4% OFF

_____ Store B

© Harcourt

Challenge CW113

Name _____

More Interest, Please!

When you deposit money in a bank, you receive interest. The bank even pays you interest on the interest they paid you. This is called compound interest.

If you invest $1,000 for two years at 5%, the bank calculates your interest in the following manner:

End of Year 1

$1,000 × 0.05 = $50.00 interest

So, you have $1,000 + $50 = $1,050 in the bank.

End of Year 2

$1,050 × 0.05 = $52.50

So, you have $1,050 + $52.50 = $1,102.50 in the bank.

Use a calculator to find the amount in the bank for each amount, using compound interest. Round to the nearest cent where necessary.

1. Principal: $3,000
   Rate: 5%
   Years: 2

   $3,307.50

2. Principal: $5,000
   Rate: 5%
   Years: 3

   $5,788.13

3. Principal: $7,000
   Rate: 6%
   Years: 4

   $8,837.34

4. Principal: $8,000
   Rate: 7%
   Years: 4

   $10,486.37

5. Principal: $12,000
   Rate: 7%
   Years: 5

   $16,830.62

6. Principal: $18,000
   Rate: 6.8%
   Years: 4

   $23,418.42

7. Principal: $24,587
   Rate: 3.5%
   Years: 10

   $34,682.39

8. Principal: $100,000
   Rate: 9.5%
   Years: 10

   $247,822.78

© Harcourt

Figure Fun

Look at each figure. Estimate the percent of the figure that is shaded.
Possible estimates are given.

1. Figure A __about 25%__

2. Figure B __about 25%__

3. Figure C __about 75%__

4. Figure D __about 25%__

5. Figure E __about 40%__

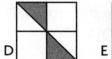

Suppose a dart lands on each figure above at random. Estimate the
probability that it lands in a shaded area. Possible estimates are given.

6. Figure A ____ $\frac{1}{4}$ ____

7. Figure B ____ $\frac{1}{4}$ ____

8. Figure C ____ $\frac{3}{4}$ ____

9. Figure D ____ $\frac{1}{4}$ ____

10. Figure E ____ $\frac{2}{5}$ ____

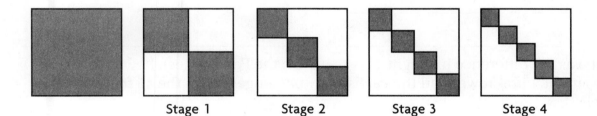

Stage 1   Stage 2   Stage 3   Stage 4

Use the sequence of figures above to answer the questions below.

11. If the large shaded square represents 1, what fractional part of
the square is shaded in Stage 1?

____ $\frac{1}{2}$ ____

12. What fractional part of the square is shaded in Stage 2? Stage 3?
Stage 4?

____ $\frac{1}{3}, \frac{1}{4}, \frac{1}{5}$ ____

13. Stage 5 is not shown. What fractional part of the square would be
shaded in Stage 5?

____ $\frac{1}{6}$ ____

© Harcourt

A True Story

You could say that in at least one way, Ferris wheels all over the world are related to the Eiffel Tower in Paris, France. The Chicago Exposition world's fair of 1893 opened a few years after a world's fair in Paris. For the Paris fair, A. G. Eiffel designed a 984 ft high tower. The tower, of course, came to be called by his name.

American engineer George Ferris was so inspired by this that he wanted to build something very large for the Chicago fair. He chose a large revolving wheel. The diameter of the wheel was 250 ft. Its supports held its 45 ft long axle 140 ft above the ground. The wheel held 36 cars around its edge and could carry 1,440 passengers at one time.

During the time the Chicago Exposition was open, about 92% of the people who came to the fair rode the Ferris wheel. Today, Ferris wheels are a common sight at amusement parks and carnivals, thanks to George Ferris.

Use the story. Write if the story has *too little*, or *enough* information. Then solve the problem if possible, or write what information is needed to solve it.

1. How many years after the Paris world's fair was the Chicago Exposition held?

   too little; need the year of the

   Paris World's Fair

2. When the passengers rode the Ferris wheel, what was the greatest height they could reach above the ground?

   enough; 140 + 125 = 265 ft

3. What was the difference in height between the Eiffel Tower and the Ferris wheel?

   enough; 984 ft − 265 ft = 719 ft

4. On the Ferris wheel, how far were the passengers from the 45 ft long axle?

   enough; about 125 ft

5. How many visitors to the Chicago Exposition rode the Ferris wheel in 1893?

   too little; need the number of

   visitors to the fair in that year

6. How many passengers could fit in each of the 36 cars around the Ferris wheel?

   enough; 1,440 ÷ 36 = 40

7. How long ago did the Chicago Exposition open?

   enough; current year − 1893

8. During the entire length of the Chicago Exposition, about how many people rode the Ferris wheel?

   too little; need the total number of

   visitors to the fair and the entire

   length of the Chicago Exposition

© Harcourt

Name _____

Odds in Favor, Odds Against

Find the odds in favor of and the odds against each event.

1.

Event: Draw an A.

Odds in favor: ___3:5___

Odds against: ___5:3___

2.

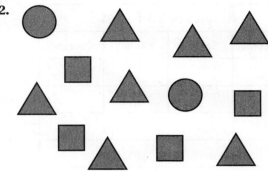

Event: Draw a circle.

Odds in favor: ___2:11___

Odds against: ___11:2___

3.

Event: Toss 2 heads.

Odds in favor: ___1:3___

Odd against: ___3:1___

4.

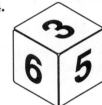 

Event: Roll a sum of 2.

Odds in favor: ___1:35___

Odds against: ___35:1___

5.

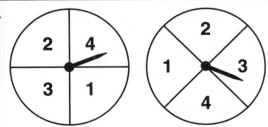

Event: Spin a sum of 5.

Odds in favor: ___4:12___

Odds against: ___12:4___

6.

Event: Spin and roll a sum of 4.

Odds in favor: ___3:21___

Odds against: ___21:3___

Three Coin Toss

Work with a partner to conduct a probability experiment.

Results of 50 Tosses

Outcome	Tallies	# Times	Percent
HHH			
TTT			
THH			
HTT			
HHT			
TTH			
HTH			
THT			

1. Toss 3 coins 50 times.

2. Record the outcome of each toss by using tally marks in the frequency table at the left.

3. Record in the third column the number of times each outcome occurred.

4. In the last column calculate the percent of times each outcome occurred.

5. Use your results to complete the table below. Use percents to compare (<, >) the experimental probability to the theoretical probability of each outcome.

Outcome	Experimental Probability	Theoretical Probability	Comparison
HHH		12.5%	
TTT		12.5%	
THH		12.5%	
HTT		12.5%	
HHT		12.5%	
TTH		12.5%	
HTH		12.5%	
THT		12.5%	

6. How do your results compare with the theoretical probability?

_____ Check students' work. _____

7. Compare the experimental probability with the theoretical probability that the outcome will be 3 heads or 3 tails.

_____ Answers will vary. Theoretical probability is 25%. _____

Decisions, Decisions, Decisions

Alfredo and Lucas are going on a camping trip. They will have to make a lot of decisions in planning this trip. Make organized lists to find out how many choices they have.

1. Alfredo and Lucas can go camping in either June, July, or August. They want to go to either Bear Mountain, Crystal Lake, or Eagle Falls. How many choices do they have?

   _____ 9 choices _____

2. Alfredo packs black, brown, and tan boots; a blue pair and green pair of hiking shorts; and a red shirt and yellow shirt. How many different outfits consisting of boots, shorts, and shirts does he have?

   _____ 12 outfits _____

3. Alfredo and Lucas can rent a regular tent or an insulated tent. There are 3 levels of down sleeping bags to choose from. How many choices of tents and sleeping bags are there?

   _____ 6 choices _____

4. When the boys arrive at the campgrounds, they find that camp-sites 10, 12, 14, 15, and 26 are still available. With each campsite they can have either firewood or a charcoal grill. How many campsite choices do they have?

   _____ 10 choices _____

5. A hiking trail splits into two trails. One of the trails is for easy hiking and the other trail is for rough hiking. Each trail goes to Natural Meadow, Beaver Pond, Eagle Point, and Scraggs Plateau. The boys want to take one of the trails to one of the sites and stop for lunch. How many choices of trail and site do they have?

   _____ 8 choices _____

6. Alfredo and Lucas are thinking about hiking back to the camp-site. They think they should leave at 4:00, 4:30, 5:00, or 6:00. They can take an easy trail or a rough trail back. They want to stop at either Natural Meadow, Eagle Point, or Scraggs Plateau on the way back. How many choices do they have?

   _____ 24 choices _____

© Harcourt

Compound Events

Elizabeth's school has 8 entrances, 6 staircases, 64 windows, and
32 classrooms. Use this information about Elizabeth's school to answer 1–8.

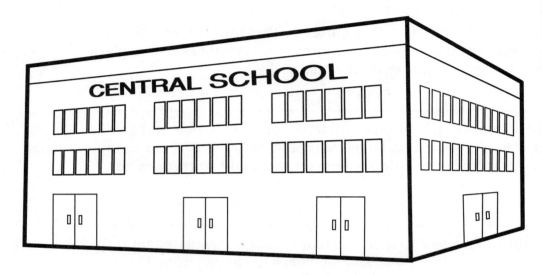

In how many different ways is it possible for Elizabeth to do the following?

1. Enter the school through one door and leave the
   school through a different door? _____56 ways_____

2. Enter and leave the school through any two doors? _____64 ways_____

3. Go up to her classroom by one staircase and come down
   for lunch by another staircase? _____30 ways_____

4. Go up to her classroom and come down for lunch
   using any two staircases? _____36 ways_____

5. Go into one classroom for her morning classes and go
   into a different classroom for her afternoon classes? _____992 ways_____

6. Have her morning and afternoon classes in any
   two classrooms? _____1,024 ways_____

7. Open one window in the morning and close a
   different window in the afternoon? _____4,032 ways_____

8. Open and close any two windows in the building? _____4,096 ways_____

9. Explain why the answer to each even-numbered problem above is
   greater than the answer to the previous odd-numbered problem.

   _____Possible answer: The even-numbered problems allow_____

   _____for repeats. The odd-numbered problems do not._____

© Harcourt

Permutations and Combinations

Benito has 7 boxes of cereal on his kitchen shelf. Every morning he combines different cereals to make his breakfast. On some days he cares about the order in which he pours the cereal into a bowl. On other days it is not important to him.

How many different permutations of breakfast cereals are possible in each situation?

1. Benito uses 2 different cereals to make his breakfast.   42 permutations

2. He uses 3 different cereals to make his breakfast.   210 permutations

3. He uses the box of Flakes first and then one other cereal.   6 permutations

4. He uses the box of Crispies first, then the box of Pops, and then 2 other cereals.   20 permutations

5. He uses 4 different cereals to make breakfast.   840 permutations

6. He uses a little of each of the 7 cereals.   5,040 permutations

How many different combinations of breakfast cereals are possible in each situation?

7. Benito uses 2 different cereals to make breakfast.   21 combinations

8. He uses 3 different cereals to make breakfast.   35 combinations

9. The boxes of Pops and Flakes are empty. He uses 2 of the other cereals.   10 combinations

Pick a Month

The members of the Video Club are having a drawing to determine in which month each one of them will be responsible for cleaning and restocking the video room. The months September through June are written on slips of paper and mixed in a box. Each person draws to determine his or her month. What is the probability of each of the following events?

1. The first person draws January. $\dfrac{1}{10}$

2. The first person draws a month that begins with M. $\dfrac{1}{5}$

3. The first person draws a month that ends in R. $\dfrac{2}{5}$

4. The first person draws August. 0

5. The first person draws September, and the second person draws January. $\dfrac{1}{90}$

6. The first person draws April, and the second person draws a month that begins with J. $\dfrac{1}{45}$

7. The first 2 people draw a month that ends with Y. $\dfrac{1}{15}$

8. The first 2 people draw a month that has 5 letters. $\dfrac{1}{45}$

9. The first person draws a month with 4 letters, and the second person draws a month with 5 letters. $\dfrac{1}{45}$

10. The first 2 people both draw months with 4 letters. 0

11. The first 2 people both draw months from September through January. $\dfrac{2}{9}$

12. The first person draws November, the second person draws April, and the third person draws June. $\dfrac{1}{720}$

13. The first 3 people draw months that end in R. $\dfrac{1}{30}$

14. The first, second, and third people draw months from January through June. $\dfrac{1}{6}$

15. The first person draws a month that begins with J, the second person draws a month with 5 letters, and the third person draws a month that ends with R. $\dfrac{1}{45}$

Name _____

Sandwich Sample

A sample of 6th, 7th, and 8th grade students at Lee Middle School was taken to see what types of sandwiches they preferred. The results of the sample are shown in the table at the right. The cafeteria staff planned to use the results of the sample to predict the types of sandwiches students in the three grades would buy at the school fair.

Sandwiches	Number in Sample by Grade		
	6th	7th	8th
ham and cheese	2	6	12
tuna	8	10	2
chicken salad	10	4	6

Find the probability that a 6th grade student at Lee Middle School will buy each type of sandwich. Write the answer as a percent.

1. ham _____10%_____ 2. tuna _____40%_____ 3. chicken _____50%_____

Find the probability that a 7th grade student at Lee Middle School will buy each type of sandwich. Write the answer as a percent.

4. ham _____30%_____ 5. tuna _____50%_____ 6. chicken _____20%_____

Find the probability that an 8th grade student at Lee Middle School will buy each type of sandwich. Write the answer as a percent.

7. ham _____60%_____ 8. tuna _____10%_____ 9. chicken _____30%_____

10. The cafeteria staff decided to prepare one sandwich per student. The numbers of sandwiches for the students enrolled in each grade are shown in the last row of the table below. Complete the table to show the numbers of sandwiches to be made for students in each grade. Use the probabilities computed in Exercises 1–9.

Sandwiches	6th Grade	7th Grade	8th Grade
ham and cheese	61	168	312
tuna	244	280	52
chicken salad	305	112	156
Total number of sandwiches	610	560	520

How many of each type of sandwich will the cafeteria staff make?

11. ham _____541_____ 12. tuna _____576_____ 13. chicken _____573_____

Name That Floor

The floor selection keys found in a hotel's elevator are shown. Each of the following describes a ride in the elevator.

Use integers to show how each rider's position changed. Then name the floor on which each person left the elevator. The first one is done for you.

1. Suki entered the elevator on the seventh floor. She traveled up three floors and then down five floors before leaving the elevator.

    +3, −5; fifth floor

2. Josh entered the elevator at the lobby. He went up six floors and then down two before leaving the elevator.

    +6, −2; third floor

3. Rob got on the elevator on the twelfth floor. He rode down to the mezzanine and then up four floors before leaving the elevator.

    −12, +4; fourth floor

4. Tomás entered the elevator from the garage. He rode up eight floors, down two floors, and then up another three floors before exiting.

    +8, −2, +3; seventh floor

5. Jon entered the elevator on the ninth floor. He rode up five floors, down six floors, and then down another two floors before leaving the elevator.

    +5, −6, −2; sixth floor

6. Tina got on the elevator at the lobby. She rode up to the fourteenth floor, down six floors, up four floors, and then she exited the elevator.

    +15, −6, +4; twelfth floor

7. Evan entered the elevator on the fifth floor. He rode down to the mezzanine, down to the garage, and up four floors before leaving.

    −5, −2, +4; second floor

8. Carole got on the elevator on the first floor. She rode up six floors, down to the mezzanine, and then up two floors before exiting.

    +6, −7, +2; second floor

⑭
⑬
⑫
⑪
⑩
⑨
⑧
⑦
⑥
⑤
④
③
②
①
Ⓜ Mezzanine
Ⓛ Lobby
Ⓖ Garage

© Harcourt

Sets

A **set** is a collection of objects. The objects that make up a set are called its **members**, or **elements**. A set that consists of some members of another set is called a **subset**.

Example 1: The set of odd numbers is a subset of the set of whole numbers. That means that all the members of the set of odd numbers are also members of the set of whole numbers.

The symbols "{" and "}" are used to enclose the elements of a set.

Example 2: $A = \{1, 3, 5, 7, 9\}$ and $B = \{1, 2, 3, 4, 5\}$.

Set A contains the elements **1**, **3**, **5**, 7, and 9.
Set B contains the elements **1**, 2, **3**, 4, and **5**.
Both sets contain the elements 1, 3, and 5.
Set A is not a subset of set B and set B is not a subset of set A.

You can use a Venn diagram to show how these sets are related.

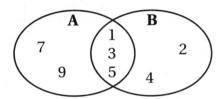

Draw a Venn diagram to show how the sets are related.

1. $A = \{2, 4, 6, 8, 10\}$ and
$B = \{1, 2, 3, 4, 5\}$
Is set A a subset of set B? Explain.

    No; the members of set A are

    not all members of set B.

2. $A = \{1, 2, 3, 4, 5\}$ and
$B = \{1, 2, 3, 4, 5, 6, 7, 8, 9, 10\}$
Is set A a subset of set B? Explain.

    Yes; the members of set A are

    also members of set B.

3. $A = \{2, 4, 6, 8, 10\}$ and
$B = \{1, 3, 5, 7, 9\}$
Is set A a subset of Set B? Explain

    No; none of the members of

    set A are members of set B.

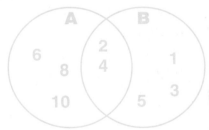

And the Number Is?

Between any two numbers there is always another number.

Place the following numbers along the path so that the numbers increase as you go along.

1.908, 1.638, ⁻0.7, 1.50, 0.534, 1.999, 1.61, ⁻0.62, 1.53, 1.732, 1.64, ⁻0.07, 1.101, ⁻0.32, 1.7, 0, 0.24, 1.887, 0.3, 1.32, 0.52, ⁻0.92, 0.562, 1.642, 0.6, ⁻0.675, 0.234, ⁻0.234, 0.675, 1.01, 1.683, 1.236, ⁻0.001, 1.3, 1.854, ⁻0.9, 1.62, ⁻0.683, 0.62, ⁻0.11, 1.69, 1.1, 1.714, 1.28, 1.86, 1.903, 0.478, 1.4, 1.45, 0.78

START

⁻1											
⁻0.92								1.1	1.101	1.236
⁻0.9	0	0.234	0.24	0.3			1.01			1.28
⁻0.7	⁻0.001			0.478			0.78			1.3
⁻0.683	⁻0.07			0.52	0.534	0.562	0.6	0.62	0.675	1.32
⁻0.675	⁻0.11									1.4
⁻0.62	⁻0.32	⁻0.234								1.45

1.683	1.642	1.64	1.638	1.62	1.61	1.53	1.50
1.69							
1.7							
1.714	1.732	1.854	1.86	1.887	1.903	1.908	1.999

FINISH | 2 |

Logically Speaking

1. Danielle, Effie, and Hannah are in the school orchestra. Each girl plays one instrument: the oboe, the French horn, or the clarinet. Hannah does not play the oboe, nor does she play the clarinet. Effie has never taken clarinet lessons. Which instrument does each girl play?

Danielle: clarinet; Effie: oboe;

Hannah: French horn

2. Austin and Koby each completed a reading assignment. Austin read more pages than Koby. Neither of the boys read more than 40 pages. The difference between the lengths of the reading assignments is 16 pages. The product of the lengths of the reading assignments is 720. How many pages did each boy read?

Austin: 36 pages; Koby:

20 pages

3. Sabrina, Tom, Carlos, and Fran like to go fishing. On one day they each caught a fish: a salmon, a tuna, a catfish, and a flounder. No one caught a fish that begins with the same letter as his or her name. Neither boy caught a salmon. Neither girl caught a tuna. One of the boys caught a flounder. What kind of fish did each one catch?

Sabrina: catfish; Tom: flounder

Carlos: tuna; Fran: salmon

4. Shandra is trying to guess Helen's secret number. Helen gives Shandra the following clues:
   • The number is between 1 and 10
   • If you divide the number by 2, the result is greater than 3.
   • If you triple the number, the result is greater than 24.
   What is Helen's secret number?

9

5. There are 12 soft drink bottles in Martha's refrigerator. The bottles are either cherry soda or root beer. If Martha takes a cherry soda and replaces it with a new bottle of root beer, there will be an equal number of each flavor. However, if she drinks a root beer and replaces it with a new bottle of cherry soda, there will be twice as many cherry sodas as root beers. How many bottles of each flavor are in the refrigerator right now?

7 cherry, 5 root beer

6. Lori, Lisa, and Lauren are sisters. When they add their ages together, they get a sum of 19. Three years from now, Lori will be twice as old as Lisa, and Lisa will be twice as old as Lauren. How old is each girl now?

Lori: 13, Lisa: 5, Lauren: 1

Name _____

Sum It Up

The integer at the top of each rectangle is the sum of four addends contained in the rectangle. Shade the boxes containing the addends you use to get the sum. You will use one addend in each row.

1.

⁻2	
+3	0
⁻9	+1
+10	⁻7
⁻16	⁻4

2.

+5	
+9	+6
⁻5	⁻7
⁻1	⁻6
+12	0

3.

⁻4	
⁻3	0
⁻8	⁻2
+10	⁻6
+3	+13

4.

+6	
+5	+4
0	+12
+6	⁻9
+4	⁻1

5.

⁻3	
+6	⁻2
⁻7	0
⁻9	+8
+8	+2

6.

0	
+10	⁻6
⁻2	+12
⁻6	⁻5
⁻9	+14

7.

+2	
+1	⁻4
+4	⁻3
+9	+2
⁻6	0

8.

⁻8	
⁻7	+2
⁻1	⁻5
⁻2	⁻4
+9	+4

9.

+4	
+5	⁻8
⁻3	⁻6
⁻2	+9
+7	⁻10

Create the Problem

Create a word problem that can be solved with each subtraction problem below. Then trade problems with a classmate, and solve each other's problems. Check students' problems.

1. $^-12 - {}^+7 =$ ___$^-19$___

2. $^+15 - {}^-9 =$ ___$^+24$___

_____

_____

_____

_____

3. $^-25 - {}^-17 =$ ___$^-8$___

4. $^-32 - {}^+14 =$ ___$^-46$___

_____

_____

_____

_____

5. $^-55 - {}^-23 =$ ___$^-32$___

6. $^+78 - {}^-19 =$ ___$^+97$___

_____

_____

_____

_____

Different Names for Numbers

Write an expression for each integer by using the integers $^+4$, $^+4$, $^-4$, and $^-4$ and any of the four operations. You can use an integer or operation more than once in an expression. An example for Exercise 1 is done for you.

Possible answers are given.

1. $^-2$ $(^-4 \div {}^+4) + (^-4 \div {}^+4)$

2. 0 $^+4 + {}^-4$

3. $^-1$ $^-4 \div {}^+4$

4. 8 $^+4 + {}^+4$

5. 24 $^-4 \times {}^-4 + {}^+4 + {}^+4$

6. 15 $^+4 \times {}^+4 - (^+4 \div {}^+4)$

7. $^-64$ $(^-4 + {}^-4) \times (^+4 + {}^+4)$

8. 2 $(^+4 \div {}^+4) + (^+4 \div {}^+4)$

9. 256 $^+4 \times {}^+4 \times {}^+4 \times {}^+4$

10. 16 $^-4 \times {}^-4$

11. 1 $^-4 \div {}^-4$

12. $^-16$ $^+4 \times {}^-4$

Name _____

Mental Properties

You can use properties of addition and multiplication to mentally
solve equations with rational numbers.

Properties of Addition	Properties of Multiplication
Commutative: $3.5 + {}^-7.4 = {}^-7.4 + 3.5$	**Commutative:** $\frac{-1}{4} \times \frac{5}{8} = \frac{5}{8} \times \frac{-1}{4}$
Associative: $\frac{1}{2} + \left(\frac{1}{4} + \frac{-2}{3}\right) = \left(\frac{1}{2} + \frac{1}{4}\right) + \frac{-2}{3}$	**Associative:** $1.2 \times (4 \times {}^-3.1) = (1.2 \times 4) \times {}^-3.1$
Additive Inverse: $\frac{-6}{7} + \frac{6}{7} = 0$	**Distributive:** ${}^-2 \times (5.2 + {}^-7.2) = ({}^-2 \times 5.2) + ({}^-2 \times {}^-7.2)$
Identity Property of Addition: ${}^-24.5 + 0 = {}^-24.5$	**Property of Zero:** ${}^-6.9 \times 0 = 0$
	Identity Property of Multiplication: $\frac{-7}{8} \times 1 = \frac{-7}{8}$

Write the property you can use to solve each equation. Then use
mental math to solve for *n*.

1. $\frac{-1}{2} \times \left(\frac{2}{3} + \frac{-4}{5}\right) = \left(\frac{-1}{2} \times \frac{2}{3}\right) + \left(n \times \frac{-4}{5}\right)$ Distributive Property; $n = \frac{-1}{2}$

2. $n + 5\frac{3}{4} = 5\frac{3}{4} + {}^-1\frac{7}{8}$ Commutative Property of Addition; $n = {}^-1\frac{7}{8}$

3. ${}^-4 \times (0.8 + 2.5) = n$ Distributive Property; $n = {}^-13.2$

4. $\frac{-5}{12} \times \frac{9}{10} = \frac{9}{10} \times n$ Commutative Property of Multiplication; $n = \frac{-5}{12}$

5. $n \times {}^-4\frac{1}{12} = {}^-4\frac{1}{12}$ Identity Property of Multiplication; $n = 1$

6. ${}^-7.8 + n = 0$ Additive Inverse Property; $n = 7.8$

7. ${}^-0.5 \times ({}^-2.2 + 4) = n$ Distributive Property; $n = {}^-0.9$

8. $n + {}^-11.7 = {}^-11.7$ Identity Property of Addition; $n = 0$

9. $n + 1\frac{5}{6} = 0$ Additive Inverse Property; $n = {}^-1\frac{5}{6}$

10. $6.2 + (3.8 + {}^-11.9) = n$ Associative Property of Addition; $n = {}^-1.9$

11. ${}^-9\frac{11}{12} \times n = 0$ Property of Zero; $n = 0$

12. $n \times 1 = {}^-30.7$ Identity Property of Multiplication; $n = {}^-30.7$

Locating Places on a Map

Many maps include a letter-number grid to help you locate places on the map. A letter-number grid is a pattern of crossed lines that form squares or rectangles. The squares or rectangles are labeled with numbers and letters at the beginning of each row or column. Use the letter-number grid on the map below to complete the activities that follow.

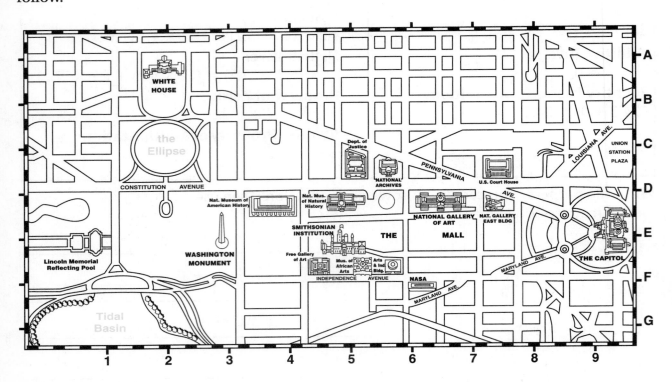

1. What famous monument is located at (E,3)?

   _____Washington Monument_____

2. What well-known building is located at (A,2)?

   _____The White House_____

3. The body of water located at (G,1) is called the Tidal Basin. Locate and label the Tidal Basin on the map.

   _____Check students' work._____

4. The circular area in front of the White House is called the Ellipse. It is located at (C,2). Locate and label the Ellipse on the map.

   _____Check students' work._____

5. Locate Pennsylvania Avenue and Constitution Avenue on the map. What letter and number could you use to tell where these two avenues intersect?

   _____(D,7)_____

6. The Capitol building is where the Congress of the United States meets. What letter and number would you use to locate the Capitol building?

   _____(E,9)_____

Name _____

Math-Ball Machines

These are special gumball machines. Examine each picture to determine the number of gumballs that will come out given the number of coins in the last picture.

1.

_____
9 gumballs

2.

_____
10 gumballs

3.

_____
27 gumballs

4.

_____
5 gumballs

Name _____

Some Things to Generalize

Write an equation to show a generalization. Then find the solution.

1. Ernesto lives on the 24th floor of a high-rise apartment building. The elevators in his building travel at the rate of 1 floor every 3 sec. How long does it take Ernesto to get to his floor, assuming the elevator doesn't make any stops?

floors (x)	1	2	3	4
time (y)	3	6	9	12

generalization _____ $y = 3x$

solution _____ 72 sec

2. Elena and two of her friends want to rent a boat on the lake. The rental fee is $3 per hr plus a fee of $5 to take the group to the launch site. What will be the total cost to rent the boat for 8 hr?

hours (x)	1	2	3	4
total cost (y)	$8	$11	$14	$17

generalization _____ $y = 3x + 5$

solution _____ $29.00

3. The local movie theater is having a sci-fi movie festival next week. The tickets are $7.50 each. Tom wants to take some of his friends so they can go as a group. He has $90 to spend on tickets. How many people can Tom take to the sci-fi festival?

tickets (x)	1	2	3	4
cost (y)	$7.50	$15	$22.50	$30

generalization _____ $y = 7.5x$

solution _____ 12 people, including himself

4. Mika wants to put a border along the top edge of the wall in her bedroom. The pattern looks like this:

squares (x)	1	2	3	4
circles (y)	2	4	6	8

generalization _____ $y = 2x$

solution _____ 16 squares, 32 circles

Mika needs to repeat the pattern 16 times. How many squares and circles will she need?

© Harcourt

It's All in the Translation

The endpoints of 12 line segments are given. Translate each segment as indicated. On the graph below, draw the translation of each segment. Do not draw the original segments. The translations will make a word.

Endpoints	Translation		Endpoints	Translation
1. (3,5), (3,⁻1)	down 1		7. (⁻9,0), (⁻12,6)	down 2, left 1
2. (6,0), (6,⁻6)	up 4		8. (0,0), (⁻3,⁻6)	up 4, left 7
3. (10,8), (10,2)	down 4		9. (⁻6,0), (⁻3,6)	down 2
4. (⁻10,⁻2), (⁻10,4)	left 3		10. (0,4), (3,⁻2)	left 3
5. (0,8), (0,2)	down 4, left 7		11. (⁻4,8), (0,8)	down 4, right 5
6. (⁻5,⁻5), (⁻1,⁻5)	up 5		12. (6,7), (10,7)	down 6

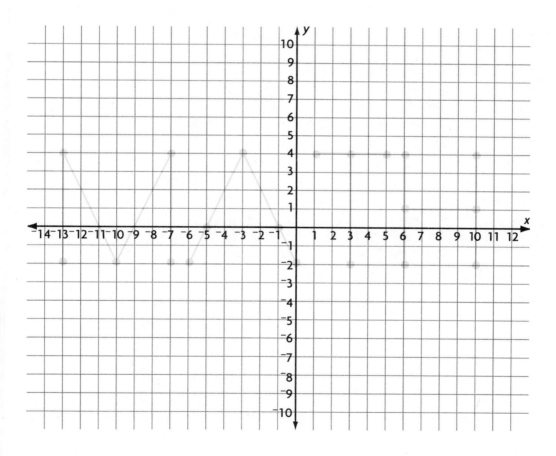